# PARAKEETS

D0112891

Printed and Distributed by T.F.H. Publications, Inc.
Neptune City, NJ

# PARAKEETS

Nikki Moustaki

T.F.H. Publications, Inc.
One TFH Plaza
Third and Union Avenues
Neptune City, NJ 07753

This book has been published with the intent to provide accurate and authoritative information in regard to the subject matter within. While every precaution has been taken in preparation of this book, the publisher and author assume no responsibility for errors or omissions. Neither is any liability assumed for damages resulting from the use of the information herein.

ISBN 0-87666-749-3

Printed and bound in the United States of America

# About This Book

*Parakeets* is an updated version of the best-selling, breed-specific bird series from T.F.H. Publications. This modernized edition of the popular guide contains the most recent information available about the breed, from housing and nutrition to taming and training techniques, as well as tips on choosing the right bird for you, behavior, natural instincts, and health care. Complemented by all-new photographs, each book in the series provides bird owners with all the advice they will need to raise a happy, healthy bird.

# *Contents*

**Parakeets remain among the most popular of all pet birds and also are among the most colorful.**

# CHAPTER 1

# An Introduction to Parakeets

Parakeets, called budgies in many countries, are the most popular companion birds in the world. There are millions of parakeet owners around the globe, which proves that there must be something special about this little bird. There are also budgie clubs and budgie shows—people take this bird very seriously.

Parakeets are relatively easy to care for and they are excellent pets for someone new to birdkeeping. Their small stature, inexpensive price, and easy-going nature also make them a beloved pet for the more advanced bird keeper or breeder. Parakeets are intelligent, full of antics, and they are great talkers, making them a popular choice for novices and fanciers alike.

Whether you have one already and want another, or whether you are still doing your homework, you've come to the right place. Perhaps you have a flock of parakeets and want to learn more—that's wonderful. The more the merrier.

The parakeet, as a companion, seems to have it all. Its size and noise level make it a perfect pet for those people living in an apartment, and it lives peaceably in a colony setting for those who have more room to spare. The parakeet is a highly trainable animal, adjusts well to living with humans, and has a long history as a pet. It can be exceptionally friendly, wanting nothing more than to sit on its owner's shoulder all day and watch the world go by.

## PARAKEETS AND ENGLISH BUDGIES

Parakeet or budgie? Part of the confusion between these two is simply a question of labeling. The name *budgie* is short for budgerigar, the Australian name for the parakeet. The name *parakeet* is really a generic term for most long-tailed parrots. However, in the

**English budgies in various colors are popular birds with breeders and advanced keepers.**

United States, the term *parakeet* is used for the bird that is the subject of this book. In most of the other places in the world, the term *budgie* is used. No matter how you say it, you're talking about the same bird.

You may have noticed that there are some budgies that look like they are on steroids and have been pumping iron at the gym—these are called English budgies and are primarily exhibition birds, though many people keep them as pets. The American budgie, the common pet budgie, is really a misnomer—these birds are originally from Australia.

There are several differences between the bird known as the English budgie and the bird known as the American parakeet. Though they both originate in Australia, the American parakeet is far more similar to its wild cousin than the English budgie.

The English budgie is larger and statelier than the American parakeet. It got its English distinction from the fact that the British concentrated on breeding this bird and making it the size and shape it is today.

**Whether you call them budgies or parakeets, these colorful little parrots are easy to keep and fun companions.**

You may ask yourself why humans would want to try to improve on nature. Well, that's something we've been doing to animals ever since we learned to live with them. The process of changing the traits of an animal through selective breeding to make it more appealing or useful to humans is called *domestication*. Though no companion bird is really domesticated, the English budgie comes close.

The English show budgie seems twice the size of the American parakeet—it is stout and regal, with a proud, thrusting chest and a forehead that looks like its feathers have been teased into a pompadour. The eyes are often barely visible and the beak is tucked deeply into the feathers in its face. The English budgie is 8 to 9 inches long in comparison to the American, which is about 7 inches long. The American budgie is slighter in appearance and is more streamlined.

The temperament of the two birds is quite similar, though the American budgie is said to be more active and mischievous and the English is mellower. Both make good pets. Though you will be able to find English budgies in the pet shop, they are probably not "show quality" birds. You will have to buy a show bird from a breeder. The

You can expect a healthy parakeet to live for at least seven or eight years, with many reaching 15 years. These are not throw-away pets!

**Many keepers feel parakeets make the best of all bird pets because of their small size and ease of training.**

English budgies that you buy in the pet shop are meant to be pets—no breeder would sell a prize English budgie to a pet shop. So, if you're looking for a pet, either bird will do.

The English budgie has about half the lifespan of the American parakeet, about seven or eight years. Because many in this line of birds are the result of inbreeding, they are less resistant to congenital problems. Your American parakeet, however, can live to be 15 years of age if you take good care of it.

## COMPANIONSHIP

When a parakeet loves you there is no question of its affection. The human-parakeet bond can be a strong one. Parakeets make especially good companions when they are acquired as well-socialized youngsters. It is not easy to find a hand-fed parakeet, but some breeders are willing to hand-feed a bird for a little more money.

Parakeets that get a lot of hands-on attention become intensely bonded to their human companions. A parakeet that is left alone for too long will begin to lose its pet quality and may become indifferent or nippy.

The parakeet shows its affection to its human companion by doing a number of odd behaviors. It will preen its human's hair and will try to kiss its human on the mouth (this is not recommended, as the human mouth contains bacteria that aren't good for a parakeet). A male parakeet will often regurgitate to its human as a sign of ultimate affection—the notion of vomiting as affection is ghastly, but it's actually a very charming gesture. An affectionate parakeet will hide in its human's clothes or underneath long hair and may even fall asleep there—that's a sign that your parakeet is very comfortable with you.

## INTELLIGENCE

The parakeet is an intelligent individual, able to figure out how to escape from its cage or a box and able to get you to do its bidding pretty quickly using vocalizations and other behaviors. Some parakeets even take well to trick training and can learn a few impressive tricks. You'll have to evaluate your individual parakeet to see if it has the aptitude for complicated tricks. Many of the tricks you will be able to teach your parakeet are "passive" tricks, such as having the bird ride in a little car.

**Parakeets love companionship, human or bird, and live longer, happier lives when they get lots of attention.**

If kept as a pair, parakeets may give more attention to each other than to their owner.

## NOISE LEVEL

A parakeet is not a noisy parrot, but noise is a subjective thing. Parakeets will rarely annoy neighbors the way a conure or a macaw might, though a parakeet in full squawk can cause quite a racket, though the racket is not ear-piercing at all. It's more like an insistent jibber-jabber filled with chirps and whistles.

The more parakeets you have the noisier they will be. One parakeet will chatter and whistle to you; two will whistle more and call each other; more than two and there will be whole conversations going on—it may be difficult to hear yourself think.

## MESS

As with most parrots, parakeets are messy. There will invariably be seeds scattered all over your floor. Bathing is a messy affair as well and leads to sprinkled water all over the cage and surrounding area. With most birds, waste manages to find its way into very unlikely places. If you are infuriated by mess, or are a die-hard neatnik, a parakeet may not be the pet for you. There are cage accessories and acrylic cages that help to prevent mess, but there's nothing that will eliminate it.

## EXPENSES

Even though you may purchase a parakeet for a reasonable price, it's the cage and the accessories that get you in the pocketbook. Once you make the initial purchases, however, upkeep of a parakeet (or a pair) is fairly inexpensive. Keep in mind that parakeets can be destructive, and if you don't take precautions, a single parakeet can damage antiques or other expensive items—these little birds are hardy nibblers. This is why it's important to "parakeet proof" your home before your begin living with your new pet.

Here's an idea of the potential cost of keeping one parakeet as a pet.

—Parakeet: $7.00 to $15.00 or more
—English budgie: $30.00 to $75.00 or more
—Housing: $35.00 and up
—Accessories: $60.00 and up
—Feed: $15.00 plus (a month)
—Veterinary visit (well-bird check up): $27.00 and up
—Emergency veterinary visit: $50.00 and up
—New drapes: $40.00 and up
—Restoration of priceless artwork: variable

## TIME CONCERNS

A parakeet is not a fish. This seems obvious, though many bird owners treat their birds as if all that was needed for their proper care was a daily feeding and water change. A parakeet needs a good deal of attention to maintain a certain level of pet quality and mental health. A parakeet that is ignored may become unhappy and neurotic and begin to mutilate itself by picking out or chewing its feathers or other parts of its body. Even parakeets that live in pairs need your attention. An observant owner who takes the time to notice the behavioral patterns of his or her birds is an owner who has the best interest of the birds in mind.

It takes a good bit of time to provide the daily and weekly care that a parakeet needs to remain healthy. Cage and accessory cleaning might add up to four hours or more a week. Cleaning the mess that a parakeet makes takes time. There might be occasions when you will have to cancel a social outing or take a day off of work to take your parakeet to the veterinarian in the case of an illness or accident. A person with a heavy work schedule or someone who travels frequently may not have the time required to properly take care of this pet.

**Though parakeets are not noisy, they do constantly chatter and whistle. Remember this if you are the sedate type of person who dislikes background sounds.**

## RESPONSIBILITIES

As with any pet, a certain set of responsibilities comes with living with a parakeet. These responsibilities should be welcomed—a parakeet provides its owner with 12 to 15 or more years of companionship, and an owner should be willing to provide his or her pet with what it needs to live out its life in comfort, health, and happiness.

Here's a list of the many responsibilities that come with parakeet ownership:

—Daily cleaning of the cage.

—Weekly, a more thorough cleaning of the cage and surrounding area.

—Offering fresh water at least twice a day.

—Offering and refreshing fruits, vegetables, and safe table foods daily.

—Offering safe playtime out of the cage daily.

—Watching closely for signs of illness and taking your parakeet to the veterinarian if you suspect something is wrong with it or in the event of an accident.

—Parakeet-proofing your home so that it's a safe place for your parakeet to play.

—Watching other pets closely when your parakeet is out of its cage.

—Checking the cage and toys daily for dangerous wear-and-tear.

—Making sure your parakeet is neither too warm nor too cold and is housed in a spot that is free of drafts.

## YOUR PARAKEET'S NEEDS

A parakeet's needs are easy to provide, though keeping this pet is sometimes time consuming. A parakeet needs proper housing and nutrition, time out of the cage and/or room to fly or move about, a safe place to play and toys to play with, a companion other than its owner if the parakeet is not a hands-on pet, veterinarian visits, and an observant, devoted owner—you.

Parakeets are quirky birds and have very distinct likes and dislikes. If you were to ask your parakeet its preferences, it would probably answer like this:

*I like: room to fly; a lot of time out of my cage; wooden toys; sunshine—but not too much; millet spray; to be scratched on the head (when I'm in the mood for it); material for chewing; fruits and vegetables; music (a soft jazz or classical music is nice); whistling and having my owner whistle back; scattering my seed all over the floor; shiny objects; bells; bathing in my water dish.*

*An Introduction to Parakeets*

*I dislike: drafts; cold weather; extreme heat; plastic perches; the veterinarian (though I know I have to go!); loud, sudden noises; being cooped up; being ignored; people who don't know me sticking their fingers or other objects in my cage; fumes of any kind; cats.*

## PARAKEETS AND CHILDREN

The parakeet is even-tempered and tends not to be as nippy when well socialized, making it a good pet for children. However, the parakeet's beak is tough and sharp, and little fingers can be very sensitive to the occasional nip. The parakeet may be a good pet for an older child, say, those over the age of ten, who are able to understand that the parakeet is a little individual with likes and dislikes of its own, and that it may not always want to play when the child is ready. A parakeet is more likely to be injured or killed by a child than anything else. Always supervise a child when the parakeet is out of the cage.

Children have short attention spans and may become disinterested with the parakeet over time. This is a sad situation for the parakeet, an

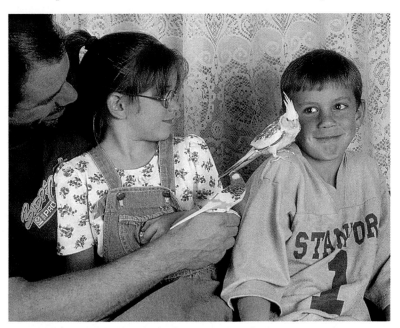

**If a child is responsible and old enough to care for a bird, a parakeet is a good choice. They are smaller than cockatiels and less expensive but no less demanding.**

animal that may bond closely with the child and will not accept being ignored. Also remember that a child will grow up during the parakeet's lifetime and may move on to other things, like college, and may not be able to take the parakeet along. A child that receives a parakeet at ten years of age might have that parakeet until she is 25!

Before a parakeet becomes a child's pet, make sure that the child understands the nature of the responsibilities he or she will have to undertake with this creature. Make a daily checklist and post it on the refrigerator or near the parakeet's cage and have the child check off the duties as they are performed. Depending on the child, you will have to make sure that the bird is actually being cared for. When you offer a pet to a child, it is important that you realize that you may have to eventually become the sole caretaker of the pet.

Parakeets are only good gifts for children (or anyone, for that matter) when it is a parakeet that the recipient desires. No child who asks repeatedly for a puppy wants to receive a parakeet—the child may become resentful of this replacement pet and take out that resentment on the bird. If you really want to give a child a pet as a gift, buy a gift certificate to your local pet shop and let your child choose his or her own pet—with limitations, of course. You could end up taking home a frog rather than a parakeet, but at least your child will have gotten the animal he or she wanted, rather than being forced to care for an unwanted pet.

If you are going to give a parakeet as a gift, don't bring the animal into the home when there's a lot of hustle and bustle, such as on a birthday or major gift-giving holiday. The bird will be confused and frightened by all of the commotion and may be neglected while the festivities are going on. Again, this is a better time to give a gift certificate, or give a photo of the gift bird and pick it up from the store when the holiday is over.

## PARAKEETS AND OTHER PETS

Parakeets can fall prey to just about any other pet you may own. A dog or cat is deadly for the little parakeet, who will be seen as prey or a toy. One little scratch during "play" is enough to kill a parakeet. Ferrets and pet rats will hunt your parakeet, and a fish tank or bowl poses a drowning threat if your parakeet is allowed free in your home. A fierce bird of another species may harm the parakeet, who won't be able to defend itself well.

**Parakeets need lots of attention, so keeping several may require more time than you want to spend. They truly are a commitment.**

If you have other pets, make sure that they either get along well, as in the case of other birds, or that they do not have the chance to "get together," in the case of dogs and cats. Never, ever think that it's "cute" to introduce your parakeet to a predator—this is just asking for trouble. A fully flighted parakeet (one without its wings clipped) may be better able to keep itself away from predators in your home, though a parakeet that has full flight can run into other dangers.

## FINAL CONSIDERATIONS

Many people think that just because they are small, parakeets cannot get lonely or anxious. This is a not true; parakeets need as much attention and care as any other bird. A lonely or mistreated parakeet can develop illnesses and self-mutilating behaviors that can be deadly. If you do take on a parakeet as a pet, think ahead to what you're going to be doing in your life. Are there going to be any major life changes? Will you be able to care for this bird in the long term? A parakeet can live 12 to 15 years or more with the proper care. What will your life be like 15 years from now? Make a solid commitment to your bird that you will care for it for the duration of its life. If you can't commit to a close relationship with a single parakeet, it's best to buy a pair—they will keep one another company and all you'll have to do is provide the proper diet, housing, and maintain an acceptable level of cleanliness.

The wild parakeet is primarily green, but many color mutations have been developed over the years.

# CHAPTER 2

# *The Wild Nature of Your Companion Parakeet*

Companion birds are not really domestic animals, even though many, such as the parakeet, have been kept in captivity for hundreds of years. Your parakeet has many things in common with its wild cousins, everything in common, in fact, except location. Your parakeet is essentially a wild bird living a very cushy life. Your parakeet's behavior, nutritional needs, and desire for companionship are all part of the wild nature of your bird.

The wild budgie feeds mainly on grasses and plant material and gets a lot of exercise, flying many miles in a day with little rest. Water is often hard to find in the parakeet's arid terrain, so finding water is often quite a task. Breeding takes place when food and water are plentiful, mainly during the rainy season.

The wild parakeet eats frequently, but it eats fresh seeds and plant material and also gets a great deal of exercise. This is far different from what your parakeet is used to. In order to give your parakeet the ideal life, you will want to make sure it eats the freshest food possible (not just dry seeds) and gets as much exercise as possible—this might mean that you provide your parakeet with a flight cage or aviary. By looking at birds' lives in the wild you can better see how to try to care for them in captivity.

## A LITTLE PARAKEET HISTORY

Budgies came to Europe around 1838 with the British naturalist John Gould and his brother-in-law, Charles Coxen, who is credited with hand-raising the first clutch of wild babies. The newly European budgies bred readily, and they soon became fancied by the wealthy people of England. Other Europeans became enamored with the species, and they became popular in Belgium, Holland, France, and Germany.

Around 1850 the budgie was displayed at the Antwerp Zoo in Belgium and it began to gain in popularity, being bred in such numbers that people other than the very rich were able to enjoy this little bird as a beloved pet.

In about 1875, a yellow mutation in the budgie occurred in Belgium, leading to other new mutations such as olive, dark green, gray-green, and light yellow. Other mutations occurred around this time as well, including pied, white-blue, and clearwings.

Pet budgies remained green until around 1881 when a Dutch bird keeper was lucky enough to discover a blue chick in the nest. From this blue bird came other mutations: cobalt, slate, gray, and violet.

Importation of budgies continued until 1894, when Australia banned export—the Europeans had to then breed their existing stock to be able to continue the hobby. Today, the budgie enjoys a healthy fancy in Europe, with new mutations being "discovered" frequently. Europeans are responsible for the English budgie, as well as for many of the beautiful budgie colors that we enjoy today.

In 1925 the budgie took off in Japan after a Japanese prince saw a pair of cobalt blue budgies in England and brought them back to his country. This began such a demand for budgies in Japan that European breeders could hardly supply enough. The Japanese soon began breeding budgies too.

The budgie came to American around the late 1920s but didn't experience real popularity until the 1950s, which saw "two parakeets in every home." Many people remember with nostalgia their first feathered pet—a pretty parakeet.

Today there are over 70 recognized color variations stemming from that simple green Australian budgie, and many other colors aren't even recognized yet. Even with the many colors available, most Americans want the most common, basic colors: green, blue, yellow, and white—these are the colors that you will find in the pet shop. You'll have to look for a breeder if you want the fancier colors.

## PARAKEETS IN THE WILD AND IN CAPTIVITY

The parakeet enjoys a very wide natural range on the Australian mainland. The wild parakeet is found in large flocks and is highly nomadic, always searching for water. Parakeets are capable of flying hundreds of miles in search of a source of water. They breed in the rainy season when water and food are most readily available and nest in hollowed out trees or tree limbs. The wild parakeet is a bit smaller than the domestically-bred parakeet and occurs only in the

**Blue parakeets are very popular and were one of the first color mutations developed.**

wild green color. This color helps the wild parakeet to blend into its habitat. Hawks and other raptors often prey upon them, so camouflage is extremely important.

The parakeet's scientific name is *Melopsittacus undulatus*, which, roughly translated, means "song parrot with wavy lines." The common parakeet, called the *budgerigar* in Australia, has been known over the years by many different names: American parakeet, English budgie, undulated grass parakeet, zebra parakeet, and the warbling grass parakeet, to name a few. They have even been called lovebirds, but are not to be mistaken for the real lovebirds, which originate in Africa.

Your parakeet is a captive-bred bird, meaning that it was not imported from the wild, but was bred in captivity. The parakeet breeds very well in captivity, so there is no reason to import them from the wild. The ban on bird importation requires that all birds being sold today are either captive-bred or were brought into the US prior to 1991.

**Parakeets are sold with leg bands coded to identify the breeder, birthdate, and other information. Only a veterinarian should remove a band.**

*The Wild Nature of Your Companion Parakeet*

It is likely that your parakeet has a metal band on its leg. This closed band has information about your bird etched into it, including the initials of the breeder, the state where the bird was bred, the year the bird was hatched, and a number that is unique to your individual bird. This number helps the breeder keep records of the babies. Some pet owners have this band removed, especially if it is irritating the bird or there is a chance that the band will become caught on something in the cage or aviary, causing injury to the bird. Never try to remove this band yourself or you might break your parakeet's leg. Your avian veterinarian has a special tool to remove the band. However, if you remove the band, you will have no way of identifying your bird should it fly away.

## EATING HABITS OF THE WILD PARAKEET

The wild parakeet consumes a variety of plant material. They feed primarily on the ground and are notorious for raiding farmers' grain fields, making them quite pesky in their native land. Because of the parakeet's ability to forage and to go for periods of time without a good water supply, they are hardy birds in captivity, where food and water are abundant. No wonder the captive parakeet is prone to obesity! Even though young seeds are a main staple of the wild parakeet, dry seed should only be a small part of your captive parakeet's diet. Too many seeds can lead to malnutrition and obesity

The wild parakeet feeds mainly in the hour just after dawn and again in the hour just before dusk. This is the time when your pet parakeet is the hungriest. You can capitalize on this natural behavior by feeding the most nourishing foods at this time and by limiting seeds.

## THE IMPORTANCE OF EXERCISE

The wild parakeet is an active bird whose days are filled with flying, foraging for food, playing, avoiding predators, finding nesting sites and nesting, protecting the nest, and raising young. No doubt your companion parakeet does not have this much to do. Pet parakeets are prone to become too heavy, which can lead to fatty tumors and even a greatly reduced lifespan. To help your parakeet remain fit and trim, provide it with as much exercise as possible. Flying is wonderful exercise, perfectly suited for birds, but it is not always advisable to have a parakeet flying inside the average home. A parakeet with its wings clipped can get exercise from flapping, playing with toys, climbing ropes and ladders, and plenty of playtime out of

Playing with toys of all kinds is a natural behavior for a parakeet and also good exercise. Be careful with frayed ropes, however.

the cage with its owners. Walking around on the floor might seem like good exercise for your bird, but there is a risk that it can be stepped on (especially if your carpet and your parakeet are similar in color) or become a snack for the family dog or cat. Short training sessions are also good exercise for your parakeet, who will have to concentrate on moving and learning something new.

## WILD BEHAVIORS IN YOUR COMPANION BIRD

Your parakeet has a lot in common with its wild cousins. Even though the parakeet is an animal that has been kept in captivity for many years, it is not domesticated and still has all of its natural instincts. These are behaviors that are difficult or impossible to "train out" of your bird. They are programmed into its bird brain and no amount of training will help. But that's okay—there are things you can do to prevent or discourage annoying behaviors. Above all, remember that your bird, like you, just wants to be itself. Don't expect too much from your parakeet. It is just being a bird the only way it knows how.

The wild behaviors that your pet parakeet is prone to do (and that may irritate or dumbfound you) include:

### The Wild Nature of Your Companion Parakeet

*Vocalizations:* Wild parakeets vocalize insistently around dawn and dusk, and then chirp and jibber-jabber pretty much all day long as they go about their business of finding food and courting. Your pet parakeet will do the same. You will not get your parakeet to stop vocalizing, but you can choose the time in which it begins its daily routine. However, if your parakeet is already used to vocalizing at a certain time of day, no amount of darkness will help—birds have very good internal clocks and will be able to tell when it's time to whistle up a storm.

*Finding a high spot:* Birds like to sit in the highest spot possible because a high place makes a good, secure lookout point. Birds are prey animals, and as such, are always on the lookout for predators. You may find that your parakeet stops vocalizing when your dog or cat enters the room, or becomes agitated when it sees a hawk over-head, even if there's a window between it and your bird. Because parakeets forage on the ground, they are extra sensitive to sound and movement. You may find that your parakeet likes to sit on the ceiling fan (watch out!) or on your curtain rods. There's not much you can do to remove this behavior, so buy a playpen and place it in a high spot where your bird will feel comfortable.

**A parakeet naturally wants to get to the highest spot around, so many toys allow it to climb to the top of the cage.**

*Sexual behaviors:* Even a single parakeet has the natural instinct to breed and will try it with a toy, a coop cup, or its owner's hand. A parakeet that is stimulated to breed may also become cranky and nippy during this time. In the wild, parakeets breed when there's an abundance of light, food, and water. Your parakeet has the same programming. If your parakeet will not give up its breeding behavior, cut down the amount of light it receives to about eight hours a day, serve water in a smaller cup (to discourage bathing), discontinue bathing for a time, and remove the toy or cup your parakeet has a crush on. When the sunlight in your part of the world begins dwindling, you can go back to bathing your bird. Or, better yet, get your parakeet another parakeet as a friend.

## THE MANY MUTATIONS

In the wild, there is one color for parakeets—green. You will notice, however, that there are many colors and patterns available in the pet shop or at the breeder's home. These colors are called mutations and are naturally occurring deviations from the normal color. The reason why we don't see these mutations in the wild is because

**Breeding parakeets can be complicated and is not covered here. Notice the breeding box behind the cage of this pair.**

Courting male (larger, with blue cere) and female (fleshy cere) parakeets. Sexual behavior is part of the life of any parakeet.

a wild parakeet that is any color other than green would be an easy mark for a predator and may not live long enough to pass along its genes. In captivity, breeders single out these mutations and breed them widely so that new mutations can develop.

Because green is the most common color, it is the least expensive to buy. The more common mutations, such as lutino (yellow) and blue, are also easily found in pet shops and come with a reasonable price tag. The rare or "fancy" mutations are more difficult to find and come at a higher price, though there is no difference in pet quality among the many mutations.

**Relatively large and expensive English budgies often are available but are not significantly better pets than the common parakeet; they are of course the same species.**

CHAPTER 3

# *Choosing the Perfect Parakeet*

Choosing the perfect parakeet might seem easy—just visit your local pet shop and choose the prettiest one. That's one way of doing it, certainly, but it's not the best, most informed way to choose a pet that will be a member of your family for many years. If you've already bought a parakeet on impulse, don't fret—this chapter will help you in case you want to buy it a friend.

## WHICH PARAKEET IS RIGHT FOR YOU?

There are several important decisions that go into choosing the right parakeet for your family. Not all parakeets will have the characteristics you might be seeking in a companion animal. Begin by making a list of all of the factors that you wish for in a pet bird. For example, some people will want a very affectionate, hands-on pet; another person is looking for a pair of birds to watch and care for; and still another is looking for compatible aviary birds. Do you want to have to train your parakeet to be friendly, or do you want one that will cuddle with you the first day you own it? Do you want a bird that's going to talk well, or will you be content with one that simply whistles? Here are some factors you will want to consider.

## PARAKEET OR ENGLISH BUDGIE

You will notice, when you walk into the pet shop, that the store might have a cage pen full of chattering active parakeets and a cage with only one or two English budgies in it. These birds look remarkably the same, except for their size.

Whether you buy a standard American parakeet or an English budgie depends on what you want from a bird. Here is the basic

**These young parakeets are easy to handle without much training.**

breakdown, aside from size, of what you will get with either one of these birds:

**American Parakeet:**
Cost: $7.00 to $14.00.
*Lifespan:* 10 to 15 years.
*Temperament:* can be tamed to be very sweet.
*Breeding:* easy to breed.

**English Budgie:**
Cost: $25.00 to $75.00 (or more, depending on color).
*Lifespan:* 6 to 8 years.
*Temperament:* can be very sweet.
*Breeding:* not as easy to breed successfully as the American parakeet, but not as difficult as some other commonly kept parrots.

The English budgie will need a larger cage, but aside from that, and the difference in lifespan, either choice will make a good pet.

## HAND-RAISED OR PARENT-RAISED?

A hand-raised parakeet, that is, one that has been taken out of the nest when it was young and handfed by a human, makes a better

Semi-tame parakeets are easily trained using compassion and patience.

initial hands-on pet than a parent-raised parakeet does, though it's not easy to find hand-raised parakeets. Because of their low cost, most breeders consider handfeeding them a waste of time, though you can order a handfed parakeet if you know a breeder and are willing to pay a bit more. A hand-raised parakeet may want to play with its human companion right away; a parakeet that was raised by its parents will not see a human owner as a playmate and may shy from contact until trained. Some people handle baby parakeets in the nest and socialize them to humans in that way, rather than hand-feeding them—these baby parakeets get the best of both worlds. Young parakeets are easy to tame and train even if they never received human contact and can be handled in just a few taming sessions, so don't fret if you can't find a handfed parakeet—you're not alone—most parakeets are not sold with a lot of socialization to humans.

## AGE

If you want a very affectionate pet, it is best to buy a parakeet that is eating on its own at about six to eight weeks. An older parakeet

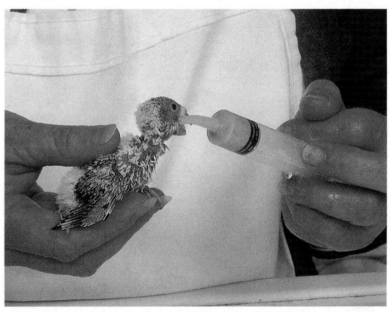

**A hand-raised parakeet is already bonded to humans and requires less adjustment to the home.**

**A lot of time is involved in hand-raising a bird, which may make them more costly than parent-raised birds.**

can make a wonderful pet as well if it has been handled regularly and is tame and sweet. Unfortunately, most pet shops do not take the time to handle their parakeet stock, so the birds often "revert" as they grow older and lose the ability to be handled easily. No matter—a few training sessions with an older parakeet should being it around.

## COLOR

No one color of parakeet is superior to another, even though the different colors often come with different price tags. Some of the mutations, such as blue or lutino (yellow), are so common that their price is comparable to the wild green color, while some other, newer mutations are far more pricey. You might find a rather "dull" looking parakeet priced much higher than a "prettier" bird—this is because parakeet fanciers prize the different mutations and because a "dull" looking parakeet can lend its genes to a mate to produce stunning babies of various colors. If you intend to breed your parakeet, you may want to invest in the rarer mutations, which you will be able to find at bird shows or through serious parakeet breeders.

## RESCUED PARAKEETS

Many animal shelters and bird rescue organizations regularly have parakeets up for adoption. You may want to put yourself on a list at your local shelter in the case that they get a parakeet in for adoption. Let your local pet shop or avian veterinarian know that you are in the market to adopt a parakeet that needs a new home. Remember that this bird might come with some quirks and will need extra patience and love in order for it to thrive in its new environment. Change is difficult for a bird, so be aware that a rescued parakeet might be anxious until it gets adjusted to its new surroundings.

## MALE OR FEMALE?

Both male and female parakeets make wonderful pets, so there's no reason to be concerned with choosing a baby bird before you know its sex. Males are more prone to talk than females, though both sexes make good whistlers. Once a parakeet is mature, it is easy to tell the difference between the sexes. Take a look at the fleshy area just above your bird's beak—this area is called the cere. When the parakeet is immature, the cere is white or pinkish. Once the bird has come into full maturity at about five to seven months of age, the male's cere will be blue and the female's cere will be pink or brown.

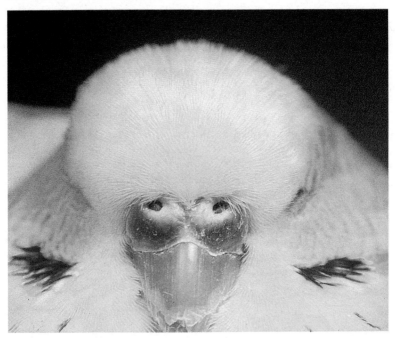

**Adult male parakeets have a bright blue cere, the fleshy area around the nostrils.**

**The fluffed head feathers of the male parakeet are normal for displaying males.**

## NUMBER OF BIRDS

A single parakeet can make a better hands-on pet than parakeets kept in a pair, though most well-trained parakeets do not lose their pet quality when kept with other birds. Parakeets in pairs are less likely to mimic human speech than the single parakeet, so keep that in mind if you want a talking bird. In the case of a single parakeet, you act as its "mate," providing the love and affection it needs to be happy. Keeping one parakeet alone in a cage with no human or bird contact is cruel. If it happens that your pet is not getting the attention you once provided due to a lifestyle change, consider getting it a friend.

## WHERE TO ACQUIRE YOUR PARAKEET

For many people, the parakeet is an impulse buy from a pet shop. Often, buyer's remorse sets in once the owner learns of all the details involved with caring for a bird, the bird gets aggressive and bites, or it becomes ill and dies due to the purchase having been made at a non-reputable store. Buying the right parakeet, one that's healthy and properly socialized to humans, is easy once you've found a shop or a breeder who cares for their young birds correctly.

Most pet shops carry a variety of birds along with their other animals. The store employees may not have a vast knowledge of birds

In an adult female parakeet the cere is flesh-colored, pinkish to tan.

*Choosing the Perfect Parakeet*

**Most parakeets are bought in pet shops or bird shops. Be sure the store is clean and the bird is healthy before purchasing it.**

and may not know much more about a particular bird than its price. The staff at a large general pet shop may not be able to recognize the signs and symptoms of illness in a bird, will know little about the history of a particular bird, and will not have spent much time playing with the birds in their care. If you buy your parakeet from a general pet shop, the responsibility might be on you to choose the best bird of the bunch, though some larger stores do employ staff to deal exclusively with their bird stock. If you sense that the employees are knowledgeable about birds, the birds seem well cared for, the cages are clean, and all of the birds have fresh food and water, then it may be safe to make the purchase there.

Pet shops that keep their birds in unclean conditions, locked away in tiny cages, are more likely to sell you an ill bird that has not been properly socialized or that has lost its pet-ability. In this case, buyer beware.

A shop that sells only birds and bird supplies might be a better place to find your parakeet. The staff in the bird shop deals only with birds and troubleshoots bird problems with customers all day long. They are trained to know how an ill bird behaves and may know something about the history and personality of your particular bird. Often, bird shops are willing to provide a new owner with a health guarantee and require a visit to the veterinarian to make the guarantee complete. It is heartbreaking to purchase a parakeet only to have it die in the first few weeks of ownership. This is why a visit to the veterinarian soon after the purchase is so important—it will show that the place of purchase is responsible for any illness the parakeet may have brought home with it. Always ask for a health guarantee before buying a bird, and get it in writing before you leave the store.

Perhaps the best place to buy a parakeet is from a parakeet breeder, one who is involved in the parakeet fancy, someone dedicated to the species and knowledgeable about the care and training of these birds. Since parakeets are not difficult to breed, you can often find a reputable breeder by looking in the classified ads in the newspaper, in the advertising section of a bird magazine, or by going to a bird show or exposition. A parakeet breeder is more likely to have the fancier mutations and might be willing to help mentor you through the trials of parakeet ownership. This is someone who cares about the lives of their baby parakeets and will be available to answer any questions you might have about raising your new feathered friend.

A bird rescue organization is a great place to go if you want to give a home to a parakeet that has been given up for adoption. Sadly, most birds typically only live in a home for two years before they are shuffled along to the next place, and as a result, there are plenty of homeless birds needing a family to call their own. Do an Internet search on "rescue birds" or call your local shelter to have your name put on an adoption list.

## HOW TO CHOOSE A HEALTHY PARAKEET

A healthy parakeet is busy and energetic, bright, attentive, active, and presents a good attitude. A healthy parakeet sings and chirps, has bright eyes, clear nares (nostrils), clean vent, and the feathers are tight and shiny. The feathers should cover the entire bird and there should be no patches missing. The bird's feet are clean and intact and it eats with gusto. The bird clambers around the cage, hops from perch to perch, and seems lively in general. When it sleeps it should do so on a perch, usually sitting on one leg. Choose a parakeet that has these qualities.

A parakeet that is not feeling well may be fluffed up and sitting on the cage floor in a corner, looking depressed. It may have a discharge from its eyes or nares and a messy vent. Its feathers might be

*Choosing the Perfect Parakeet*

**Even in the pet shop, healthy parakeets are active birds. Get a health guarantee with any purchase.**

dirty from lack of grooming and it may even have patches of feathers missing. It may appear sleepy and droopy, puffing its feathers to keep in its body heat. This is not a parakeet you want to take home, even out of pity. Let the store manager know that you believe something is wrong with this bird. It's not a good idea to buy other birds from the same store if you suspect they are selling an ill bird—many avian diseases are airborne and need no direct contact to be passed from bird to bird. Do not overlook the bird that is simply unhappy or being picked on, however—this bird may just be miserable in its present circumstance and may have feathers missing because the others are picking them out. Watch the cage dynamics closely to determine if this bird is ill or simply not suited for the hard life of a bird waiting in a pet shop for a good home.

## HEALTH GUARANTEE

Always inquire about a health guarantee and get one in writing whenever you acquire a bird. If the place you want to buy the bird from does not offer a guarantee, do not purchase your bird there. A health guarantee may require that you visit the veterinarian within a specified number of days—and that's a good incentive to take your new bird to the doctor for a check up.

**Many traditional parakeet cages really aren't suitable for these birds. They have dangerous doors and not enough horizontal wiring for climbing.**

# CHAPTER 4

# *Housing Your Parakeet*

Many people don't like the idea of keeping a bird in a cage—birds are supposed to be free, right? Yes, that's true, but the home offers many dangers for your curious parakeet. A cage will keep your bird safe and out of mischief when you're away. Supervised out-of-cage time is a necessary part of your parakeet's life, but an unsupervised parakeet might get in harm's way—and fast! Parakeets housed in the proper kind of cage with the appropriate accessories often love their cages and think of them as Home Sweet Home. A cage is not meant to be a prison, but is a safe space for your bird to reside while you're unable to supervise it.

## IMPROPER HOUSING: BUYER BEWARE

To begin a discussion of proper cages, we should first take a look at improper cages. Bamboo or wooden cages made to house finches and canaries are attractive but unacceptable for the parakeet. Cages shaped like pagodas are too tall and narrow for the parakeet, who likes a lot of horizontal space to clamber around in—cages with more vertical space than horizontal space are wasted on the parakeet. Tiny, ornate, showy cages are inappropriate as well—these are best for wooden birds. Elaborate scroll-work on a cage can catch toes or leg bands, causing serious injury. Cages whose bars are painted or covered with plastic or other materials are a terrible choice for the parakeet, who will spend the day picking the material off of the bars. The plastic material may be toxic or otherwise harmful and can cause death if ingested.

Cage bars should be spaced such that your parakeet will not be able to poke its head through them. It might not be able to get its

**Buy a cage for how comfortable it will make your parakeet, not how it will appear as a designer item. Many types are available, but some are simply not well-designed.**

head out again. A parakeet with its head stuck will panic, which can lead to a broken neck or strangulation.

## FINDING THE RIGHT CAGE

The right kind of cage isn't hard to find if you know what you're looking for. Any pet shop should carry appropriate housing for your parakeet, but you may have to pick through the selection to find what you want. Don't allow the pet store staff to push you into buying something you feel is inappropriate for your pet. A cranky, confined parakeet will be harder to train than one that's happy in its home.

## PROPER SIZE

Wild parakeets spend most of their days winging around the scrublands, searching for water, nesting, and foraging for food. A companion parakeet lives a far different life, but its energy level can surely compete with its wild cousins'. Because of their high energy level, parakeets need a large space in which to spend their days. Unfortunately, most store-bought cages are tiny and don't allow the parakeet to expend this energy, which can be turned upon itself in

Make sure the cage is big enough not only for your parakeet but also for its toys, such as swinging perches, ropes, and bells.

the form of self-mutilation. Buy the largest cage your budget and space demand. If the cage looks like it would generously house several parakeets, it might be the one to purchase.

A parakeet forced to spend its days housed in a very confined space will be extremely unhappy. Remember, birds are creatures of boundless space, and even though your parakeet was raised in captivity, its instincts tell it that being confined is unnatural. If your parakeet is going to spend a good portion of the day housed in a cage, be sure that you buy the largest that your space and budget can afford. The minimum length for a parakeet cage should be at least two feet (24 inches), though the width and height can vary from 24 inches to as large as you want. Your bird should be able to actually fly from perch to perch—this means that it should take wing-power to get from one side of the cage to the other. Most "parakeet" size cages only allow a wing-assisted hop or force the bird to clamber on the bars to move around—this size cage is too small.

## PROPER SHAPE

The perfect shape for a parakeet cage is a large square or a large, long rectangle. Corners in a cage will make a parakeet feel comfortable and give it a tight space to crawl into when it's feeling insecure or sleepy. The bars on the parakeet's cage should be primarily horizontal, with a few vertical bars for structural purposes. Horizontal bars allow the parakeet to climb around its cage and hang safely on the side.

## PROPER MATERIALS

The proper material for a parakeet cage is uncoated steel or another non-toxic metal. Many cages come in a combination of metal and plastic, which is fine for the parakeet. Acrylic cages are a nice choice for the parakeet because the solid walls prevent mess, though they don't allow for climbing and can be quite pricey. If you are going to make a cage, be sure to scrub the caging materials well and leave them outside to air out for a few weeks before you use them, because wire is often coated in zinc, which is deadly for birds.

## SAFE DOORS

Commercially-made cages commonly come with three types of doors. The best types of doors for the parakeet are the doors that open downward (like an oven door) or to the side (like your front door). Doors that slide up and down (like a guillotine) are the most common type but can cause your bird serious injury. If your cage does have this style of door, consider buying spring clips or another type of lock so that your bird can't slide the door up.

## THE CAGE BOTTOM

The proper cage for a parakeet is one that has a grating or a grill on the bottom so that the parakeet is prevented from rolling around in its own mess. In the wild, parakeets are never exposed to their own fecal materials the way they are in a caged environment. You should take care that your parakeet is exposed to as little of its own waste material as possible—a grate on the bottom of the cage will help.

## CAGE ACCESSORIES

Now that you've gotten the proper cage, you've got to furnish the cage with all of the necessities and goodies that your parakeet will need to be happy and healthy. Many of these are one-time purchases and should last the lifetime of your bird.

**Starter kits often are sold, but they may contain items you do not need or that might actually be dangerous to a parakeet. Consider all purchases carefully.**

## PERCHES

Most commercial cages come with a couple of smooth wooden dowels as perches, which are fine to use, but they are an inadequate selection for a parakeet, who spends most of its life on its feet. A wide variety of perches can help to maintain your parakeet's foot health. A parakeet that stands on the same perch day after day may develop foot sores and lameness, among other foot disorders. These are easily remedied by offering various perches made of assorted materials in many different dimensions. Your parakeet should have perches that make him stand with his feet very spread out (almost flat) and perches that allow his toes to almost touch one another when he's gripping them. Fortunately, there are many different types of perches on the market, and they are easily found at your local pet store. Buy perches made of different types of wood, rope, and concrete for optimum foot health. A parakeet with painful feet is less likely to be easily trainable than one whose feet don't hurt.

The sandpaper sheathes that slip over perches are not the same as concrete perches and, in fact, are prone to causing foot problems. The sandpaper is abrasive and can cause sores, and the paper tends to get wet and hold bacteria in it—not something you want under your parakeet's feet.

**Perches of many types are available, but natural wood of various diameters still is the best type. For healthy birds, use several types of perches in any cage.**

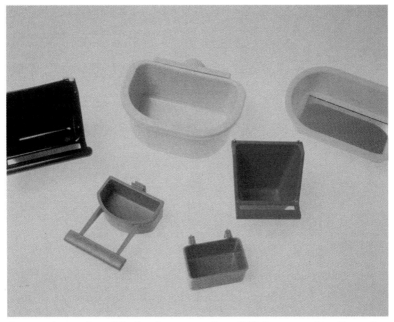

A tremendous variety of food and water cups is available in any pet shop. Remember that parakeets will rapidly destroy most plastic cups, so go with steel.

## CUPS

The standard commercial cage usually comes with two square plastic cups designed to fit neatly into doors located toward the bottom of the cage. These cups are fine, but they are by no means the best choice. Plastic cups are difficult to clean, not only because the square shape does not allow thorough cleaning of the crevices, but because the plastic eventually becomes scratched and bacteria like to hide out in the scratches and muck up the water. A standard cage usually has places for the cups at the lower half of the cage, which might allow waste to fall into the cups, which is not sanitary.

Replace the plastic cups with two sets of round, stainless steel cups—this means that you will have six cups—two for water, two for seed/pellets, and two for fresh foods. Only use one set at a time, and allow the other set to be thoroughly washed and dried before its next use. Stainless steel is easy to clean and is very durable. Ceramic cups are nice, but they are easier to break and will eventually scratch.

Some people use water bottles or self-watering tubes to dispense water. These have the disadvantage of becoming clogged or dirty,

Parakeet toys should be colorful, safe, and designed to keep your bird interested and amused. Check fittings and ropes often to help avoid accidents.

and owners tend to refresh the water less frequently. A coop cup filled with clean water at least twice a day should do nicely—no need for bottles or tubes.

## TOYS

Toys are a must for the high-energy parakeet—a parakeet without toys to fling, chew, and snuggle with will be a bored and unhappy parakeet, indeed! The single parakeet, especially, must have many toys to play with; a pair or colony of parakeets will still enjoy playing with toys but it is not necessarily essential for them to have as many. Toys give your parakeet something to do while you're away and offer much-needed exercise to a cage-bound bird.

*Safety first* is the motto when it comes to toys for your parakeet. Beware of toys that are flimsy or have small spaces where a toe can catch. Your parakeet's head should never be able to fit in a ring that comes on a toy. Toys that are made for much larger or smaller birds should never be considered. Toys labeled for parakeets and cockatiels are usually appropriate. Rope toys and perches should be trimmed regularly once they begin fraying.

*Housing Your Parakeet*

Parakeets adore swings, so make sure that you provide your pet with at least one. Mirror toys are good for the single bird, but if you notice your parakeet becoming too attached to its reflection you might want to take that toy away and replace it with something else, or your parakeet might prefer its "mirror mate" over you.

Rotating your parakeet's toys is a great way to keep them "new" and allow you time to clean them. Buy more toys than will fit in the cage at any one time and rotate them in and out of the cage on a weekly basis. Don't remove your parakeet's absolute favorite toy, however, as this can cause undue stress. Don't worry that toys will interfere with training—they don't.

## OTHER ACCESSORIES

Now that you've taken care of the essential cage accessories, here's a list of other indispensable items that your parakeet will need to thrive:

*Bird lamp:* If you live in a northern climate that is dark for much of the year or your parakeet lives in a room that doesn't get much light, you should invest in a bird lamp. There are many available on the market, or you can simply buy a spotlight from a hardware store and

**Any pet shop will have a wide variety of toys suitable for parakeets. Just keep in mind potential dangers involved with loose ends, small parts, and edible constructions.**

equip it with a bird or reptile bulb from your local pet store. This high-spectrum bulb provides your parakeet with the "natural" light it needs to maintain its health. A bird kept without the proper lighting can become malnourished. You can keep the light on for nine to ten hours a day.

*Cage cover:* Your parakeet does not need its cage covered at night, though people who like to sleep a little later in the morning might do well to invest in a dark cage cover. A cover also serves to keep out drafts and to quiet noisy birds during the day. Don't use the cover, however, for extended periods of time in daylight hours—it should only be used for a few minutes to calm noisy birds in the event that you need them to be silent, for example, when an infant is taking a nap. Be careful that the cover does not become frayed. If the cover is very thick, the extreme darkness in the cage may frighten a parakeet and cause it to thrash around its cage, a phenomenon common to parakeets—in the case that you hear flapping or distress in the cage when you cover it at night, flip up a corner of the cover and let some light through.

*Nightlight:* If your bird becomes frightened at night or you have a cat roaming the house, you will want to keep a nightlight on in your bird room. This will give your parakeet a sense of security—it will be able to tell the difference between a real predator and someone making a midnight snack in the kitchen.

*Mineral block and cuttlebone:* These items provide much needed calcium to your parakeet's diet and are fun to chew and destroy. Make sure that your bird has at least one of each, and replace them when they become soiled.

*Flooring:* Your parakeet's cage should have a metal grating on the bottom so that it can't get to its mess, but you will need to put something in the bottom of the cage nonetheless. Regular newspaper is the easiest choice, and if you change it at least every other day, it's sanitary. Many people use corncob or other types of litter for the cage bottom, but these tend to hold moisture.

*Bath:* Your parakeet will want to bathe and will do so in its water dish, unless you provide it with a special bath. There's no stopping your bird from bathing in the water dish, but a larger, shallow bath offered several times a week might help.

*Playgym:* Your parakeet will appreciate a cage-top playgym, complete with ladders and toys and even a cup for snacks.

*Seed catchers:* A cage bloomer or plastic seed guard goes a long way toward keeping seed inside the cage.

Corncob and walnut shell litters often are used in the tray of a parakeet cage to catch droppings, but they can hold moisture and become fungused if not changed frequently.

*Mite protectors*: There is no need for this item, and, in fact, the chemicals inside can be harmful for your bird. Instead of the mite protector, take your bird to the veterinarian for a check up. It's unlikely that your parakeet has mites or that it will contract them.

## HOW TO SET UP THE CAGE

1. Make sure that all of the parts of the cage are put together correctly and securely.

2. Place full food and water cups toward the front of the cage and about midway to the top. If the doors where the cups should go are too low, don't use them—use a cup holder instead.

3. Place perches at various levels toward the middle to the top of the cage, making sure that there are no perches above food or water dishes. Parakeets prefer to be at a high point in the cage, so don't position perches too low. If you place perches above one another, they are going to become soiled.

4. Place the cuttlebone and mineral block on the sides of the cage near a perch. Don't place these items too low where they can be soiled.

Parakeets hop right into their feed cups to eat, which means you have to keep these cups very clean at all times.

5. Place toys in various spots around the cage, making sure that they don't block the food and water dishes.

6. Use a pull out tray and add newspaper to the bottom of the cage—below the grate.

7. Add bird (or birds).

8. Place the spring clips or locks on the doors.

You're done! Your parakeet is home!

## CLEANING YOUR PARAKEET'S CAGE

Daily cleaning chores include changing the paper in the bottom of the cage, soaking the dishes in a 10% bleach solution, and making sure there are no waste deposits on the perches.

Weekly chores include disassembling the cage and cleaning it thoroughly with a bleach solution or kitchen soap and a scrub brush, scrubbing all the perches, and cleaning and rotating toys. A larger cage can be hosed down outside—remove parakeets first, of course!

Many household detergents and cleansers are extremely dangerous for your parakeet. Use vinegar as a disinfectant and baking soda as a cleanser (don't mix the two, however). A 10% bleach solution is fine as well—bleach is nontoxic to birds. Rinse and dry everything thoroughly before putting your parakeet back in the cage.

## CAGE ALTERNATIVES

Because parakeets appreciate being together and are generally peaceful among themselves and other peaceful species of birds, they make excellent colony birds and can be kept together in large aviaries. An aviary allows parakeets to do what they do best—fly. This is a wonderful gift that you can give your birds, and anyone with any amount of space can have an aviary. Once your parakeet is well trained, keeping it in an aviary setting will not damage that training, as long as you reinforce it daily.

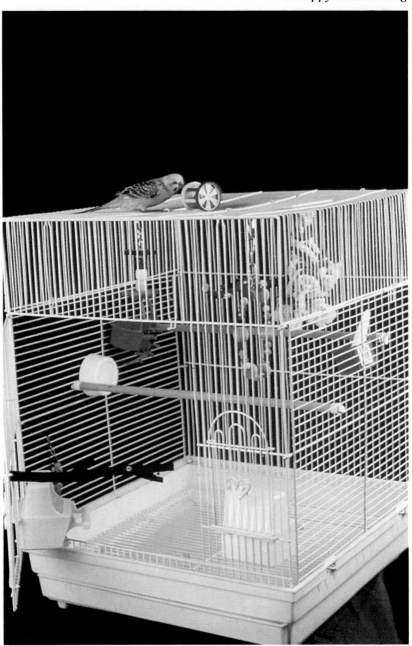

**Deciding just where to put the cage often is the hardest part of getting a parakeet settled-in. Avoid windows and areas with high traffic.**

CHAPTER 5

# A Happy Homecoming

Once you've chosen the perfect parakeet for you, there's the matter of transporting it home and setting up the ideal living situation for it. The pet shop will have cardboard boxes for you to transport your parakeet home in, but you may want to get the jump on all of the equipment you will need and buy a bird carrier, one that has grating in the front or on top so that your parakeet has a view. If you have a short ride, you don't have to bother with food and water, but if the ride is long, ask for some refreshment for your bird. Place the bird in a spot in the car that is neither too hot nor too cold, and it's best to buckle the carrier in for safety.

## PLACING THE CAGE

Where your parakeet is going to live is an important decision that can make the difference between a very happy bird and a miserable one. Your parakeet's cage is best placed in a location that gets a lot of traffic, like the family room, living room, or the room where everyone watches television. A place where there's too much swift-moving traffic, like a hallway, isn't a great location, however. The cage should be in an area where there's a sense of relative calm but the area is well attended by the members of the family.

Because your parakeet needs a good deal of attention, an out-of-the-way location isn't the best choice—it will begin to miss its "flock" (you and your family) immediately if relegated to a back room. The garage is too drafty and is prone to fumes. The bathroom and kitchen are both places that are prone to wide temperature ranges and chemicals, neither of which is healthy for a parakeet. A child's room might be dark and quiet for most of the day

**To be comfortable, parakeets need privacy and quiet as well as moderate temperatures and no drafts.**

while the child is at school and too noisy at other times. Again, the family room or television room is your best bet.

Once you've decided on the room where your parakeet is going to live, choose a corner location that is free of drafts and try to make sure that the cage is covered on at least two sides by the walls of the room, which will make your parakeet feel safe. A cage that's standing or hanging in the middle of the room will make for an extremely insecure bird. When the family cat appears or a car backfires outside, your parakeet will want to retreat to the back of the cage—a cage that's freestanding will have no "back," no place for the parakeet to "hide." To make your parakeet feel even more secure, especially if you can't place the cage next to a wall, you can surround the cage with safe, nontoxic plants. Be aware that a parakeet will make quick work of a plant, chewing it to bits, so you should carefully supervise your bird when it's out of the cage.

Don't place the cage directly in front of a window, even though this seems like the thing to do. Your parakeet really doesn't need a view. Parakeets are extremely alert creatures and will become alarmed by predators lurking outside—these predators can take the form of the

Parakeets like to have their backs to the wall, so to speak, and seldom are comfortable in a cage just hanging in the middle of the room.

neighbor's cat or dog, hawks circling in the sky, rats and raccoons, and even cars going by. The sun shining in a window may overheat your bird if it can't get out of the sunlight. It's okay for your parakeet to be placed near a window, but not directly in front of it, unless the cage is so large that part of it extends over onto a wall.

Placing a commercial cage outside on a patio or porch is extremely risky. Your parakeet will be very vulnerable to predators outside, and a cage is no match for a determined raccoon or opossum. A thief might be tempted to steal your parakeet, cage and all. The pet parakeet housed on a patio might not get as much attention as it would housed in a family room. Some people choose to house multiple parakeets in large cages on an enclosed patio or porch—in this case the parakeets have one another for company and the cage is far too large for a thief to make off with. A cage on a patio should be double-wired, that is, two layers of wire placed one over the other such that a predator would not be able to get to the feet of the birds inside—a rat or raccoon can actually pull a small bird through the wires of a cage. If you live in a place that gets very hot or very cold, house your parakeet inside.

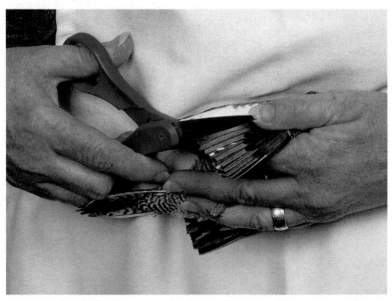

**Professionally clipping the wings of a pet parakeet not only prevents escapes, it prevents accidents as well. A flighted parakeet can get in many kinds of accidents, some fatal.**

A parakeet uses its beak to pick and chip at anything it finds curious, which includes electrical wires and even plastic and chrome coatings on cage wires.

## PARAKEET-PROOFING YOUR HOME

If your parakeet is going to have free time out of the cage and there is the possibility of you turning your back on it for a moment, even just to answer the phone, you'd better parakeet-proof your home. The average home presents many dangers for a parakeet. Here's a parakeet-proofing checklist you can follow to keep your feathered friend safe:

—Screen all windows and doors and check regularly for holes in the screening.

—Wrap all electric wires and tuck them away.

—Put decals on all windows and mirrors.

—Remove all items containing toxic metals.

—Remove all toxic plants.

—Keep toilet lids down and remove all other standing water.

—Remove ceiling fans or keep them off.

## THE MOST SERIOUS HOUSEHOLD DANGERS TO PARAKEETS

The following are the most common household dangers to the parakeet.

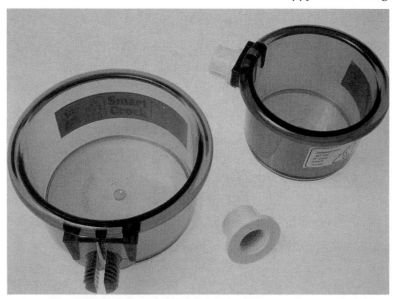

**A parakeet should be allowed to bathe only in a bowl in its cage, never in the kitchen sink where it might run into hot water, hot dishes, or cleansers.**

*Predators:* The family dog poses a huge threat to the parakeet, and the family cat is an even deadlier enemy. One slight nip from a dog, even in play, can mean death for your parakeet. Cats don't even have to bite to kill a bird—they have a type of bacteria on their claws and in their mouths that is extremely toxic to birds—one scratch and the bird will die within 48 hours unless immediate treatment by a veterinarian is sought.

*Water:* Standing water is a strong temptation for a parakeet, who may want to take a bath or drink. Unfortunately, the bird may fall into a pool deeper than it can remove itself from. Many parakeets drown in toilets, large dog bowls, fish tanks and bowls, half full drinking glasses, ponds and fountains, Jacuzzis, full sinks (with dishes soaking), and pots of boiling water—this last instance is especially awful. Keep your toilet lids down at all times, and keep all exposed water covered.

*Nonstick cookware:* Any cookware labeled "nonstick" emits an odorless fume that, when heated, can kill a bird within a matter of moments. It was previously thought that the fumes only occurred when the nonstick surface was overheated, but research now indicates that it is emitted at even low levels of heat. Birds have tremendously sensitive respiratory systems, far more delicate than ours. If you notice that your parakeet is in distress and there's no apparent reason, check for gas leaks or other fume-causing agents, such as scented candles, fireplaces, and heated nonstick surfaces.

Many items other than pots and pans can have nonstick surfaces. These include: Heat lamps, portable heaters, plates on irons, ironing board covers, stove top burners, drip pans for burners, broiler pans, griddles, cooking utensils, woks, waffle makers, electric skillets, deep fryers, crock pots, popcorn poppers, coffee makers, bread makers, non-stick rolling pins, lollipop molds, stockpots, roasters, pizza pans, and curling irons. Even a well-ventilated room isn't safe when there are nonstick items being used.

*Common household products:* Keep all household cleaning items away from your parakeet. These include soaps, drain cleaners, laundry detergents, floor cleanser, and bathroom cleaners, all of which might be a tempting treat for your parakeet—with tragic consequences. Items commonly kept in a garage should be stored away from your bird. These include fertilizers, pesticides, and barbeque

**Because of their complex respiratory system, parakeets (and other pet birds), are sensitive to most household sprays, scented candles, and heated nonstick cookware.**

products such as charcoal and lighter fluid. Realize that your parakeet can easily tear through paper bags. Items regularly sprayed into the air can cause severe respiratory distress or death, including air freshener, fabric freshener, and even scented candles.

*Toxic houseplants:* Parakeets are chronic nibblers, always shredding something to bits the moment you turn your back. Your houseplants are a serious temptation for your parakeet, who is naturally attracted to them. Even one nibble of a toxic plant can be poisonous to your parakeet and cause death.

*Ceiling fans:* Birds have a natural instinct to climb or fly to the highest spot that they can find. A high spot is generally safe from predators and is a good lookout point. A ceiling fan seems like the perfect spot for a fully-flighted parakeet. Now, imagine a parakeet flying around a room and a ceiling fan on—it's like a chicken in a food processor! One good whack from the blade of a ceiling fan is all it takes to bring your parakeet down for good. Make sure all ceiling fans are kept off or have them removed.

*Open windows and doors:* The threat of a fully-flighted parakeet winging out of an open door or window is a serious one—many parakeets that take flight outdoors are never seen again. Keep all doors and windows securely closed or screened when your parakeet is out of its cage or make sure that its wings are clipped properly. Even if you believe that your parakeet is attached to you and would never leave, or that its wings are well clipped, a loud noise such as a car backfiring might frighten your parakeet into flight and it may become confused and not find its way back.

*Feet and doorjambs:* Parakeets allowed to walk on the floor are in danger of being stepped on or crushed in a doorjamb.

*Toxic foods:* Most foods are perfectly fine for a parakeet to ingest, with the exception of avocado (parts of it are toxic), chocolate, rhubarb, alcohol, caffeine, and raw onion. These items can make a parakeet very ill or even kill it.

*Electrocution:* Some parakeets will snack on electric wires. Keep all wires wrapped and hidden away from your bird. Lamps and other plugged in appliances do not make good playgyms.

*Heavy metals:* Keep your parakeet away from stained glass decorations, costume jewelry, lead fishing weights, or other materials containing metals that can be toxic to your parakeet. Hardware cloth, the material many people use to build cages, is often dipped in zinc to prevent rusting—this zinc is deadly for your parakeet—rinse and scrub all homemade cage material thoroughly before housing birds.

## A Happy Homecoming

Many common houseplants are toxic to parakeets, so they should never be allowed in or near the cage. Monitor the parakeet carefully when it is free.

*Temperature fluctuations:* Parakeets are sensitive to extreme heat and extreme cold—they can die from overheating and are prone to frostbite in cold, windy conditions. If you live in an extreme climate, be sensitive to your parakeet's temperature requirements.

*Mirrors and glass:* A parakeet that has full flight will not know the difference between empty space and a clean window or mirror— these solid objects will look to your parakeet as if it could fly right through them, with drastic consequences. This is a great excuse to leave your windows dirty, or at least to buy pretty decals to put on them.

*Human medicines:* Never, ever try to treat your bird with human medicines, which will react very differently in your bird's delicate system than they do in yours. Treat your bird only with medicines provided by your avian veterinarian and prescribed to your bird.

### THE FIRST FEW DAYS AT HOME

When you first bring your parakeet home you will want to give it a few pressure-free days to adjust to the new environment. This is not the time to begin heavy training sessions or long playtimes away

**To keep stress to a minimum, put toys and cups in the cage before the parakeet is added to its new home.**

from the cage. Change is difficult on a bird, who is a creature that likes routine. Think of your parakeet's life before you decided to take it home—it was bred and handfed in one place, sold to another place, and now is moving to a third location—that's a lot of adjustment.

The first things to do are to set up your new friend's cage and locate it in its permanent place. This way you won't be adding toys and cups while your parakeet is simply trying to relax. Once you've placed your parakeet in its new cage and given it fresh food and water, leave it alone in quiet for a few hours so that it can get used to its new situation. Offer millet spray at this time. It's a good sign of adjustment when your parakeet begins to eat and make noise.

After a day or so you can begin taking your parakeet out of its cage for playtime. If it's a baby, gently scoop it off of the perch or side of the cage, making sure not to pull hard on its feet, which will be clutching hard to whatever it's standing on. The baby doesn't yet know to step onto your finger—you will have to teach it this command. Don't expect too much from your parakeet at first. You're both getting used to each other.

## A Happy Homecoming

Each parakeet has an individual personality and has different favorite things. You will learn all about your new bird as the days go on. In this initial stage, move calmly around the bird and play with it very gently. This is the time to build the relationship between you, the time when your bird will learn to trust you and see you as a friend. If you force an interaction at this fragile time, you may only succeed in scaring your bird, who may then remember you as someone to be feared. If you play with your bird every day for the first few weeks, perhaps even fielding a few uncomfortable nips with composure, you'll find that your parakeet will develop a sparkling, spirited personality and that the two of you will become fast friends. The change from baby bird to adolescent happens rapidly, and at about four to five months of age a parakeet begins to show how much fun it can be.

## WING CLIPPING

To properly train a bird, its wings must be clipped during the period of training or it will simply fly away from you, making training nearly impossible. Clipping a bird's wings is the act of cutting the primary flight feathers (only the outer half of the feather) so that the bird is unable to fly very high or very far. These are the only feathers on a bird that you should ever clip.

## TO CLIP OR NOT TO CLIP?

If you feel guilty about having your bird's wings clipped, you're not alone. Many people feel that wing clipping is cruel or that it hurts the bird. In truth, clipping wings, if done properly, hurts as much as a haircut, and feathers, like hair, grow back, usually in about five months if the bird is healthy, perhaps even sooner.

Should you clip your parakeet's wings? That depends more on your ideas about living with a companion bird than it does on your parakeet. No bird wants its wings clipped. Birds are creatures of boundless space. Most would take the first opportunity to dash out the window for a bit of soaring time. But then what? Your parakeet lands in a tree and sees hawks circling overhead. Cars zoom by and a neighborhood cat sharpens its claws on the trunk. Your parakeet's flying fun has now become a tragic situation. You may never find your parakeet again. And that's only one danger to keeping a parakeet flighted. Fully flighted birds are more likely to burn themselves on a hot stove, drown in the toilet, or break their necks flying headlong into clean, closed windows or shiny mirrors.

Beginners often keep their birds safer (read: alive) when they are clipped. Will your parakeet really suffer if it is not allowed to fly? Not if you give it a lot of free time out of the cage and house it in a large space. However, flying is indeed essential for the psychological well-being of a bird. This is an animal that is meant to fly, and when that's taken away, it can result in neurotic behaviors, such as self-mutilation. The bird will feel vulnerable and have little self-direction. Unfortunately, clipping is important for the safety of most parakeets, and it is especially important for training. One way to avoid neurotic behavior in your clipped parakeet is to give it as much attention as possible. You may also want to consider an aviary or habitat where your birds can fly without risk—many parakeet owners use this option and their birds are healthy and happy as a result.

Another option is to clip your new bird for an initial period of time, say six months to a year, until your parakeet is very well trained. This initial unflighted period will allow your bird to become used to you and your home, to training, to your other pets, and to other family members. You must come to know and trust your bird's habits before you make the decision to let its flight feathers grow out. Remember, the potential for tragedy is always there. If you can make your home absolutely safe, and you're positive that it can't escape or injure himself in any fashion, let it fly under supervision—it has wings for a reason. If you are not certain about your bird's safety, keep it clipped, but go the extra mile to provide the freedom and stimulation that it would otherwise get from flying.

## HOW TO CLIP YOUR PARAKEET'S WINGS

If you've chosen to clip your parakeet's wing feathers to prevent it from flying away, you should find a professional in your area that will clip them at first and show you how to do it yourself. Many owners are squeamish about clipping their own parakeet's wings and choose to have someone else do it for them. If you have an avian veterinarian, he or she is the best person to clip your parakeet's wings. That way you have the bonus of a veterinarian handling your bird. You can always clip the wings yourself and may want to learn how, especially with a parakeet, who needs the new feathers trimmed as they grow in.

When clipping wings, the first thing you must be able to do is hold your parakeet properly. You can't grab a bird any way you want, spread out a wing, and clip. This can be very dangerous and lead to injury. A parakeet has fragile bones that can break if you're too

## A Happy Homecoming

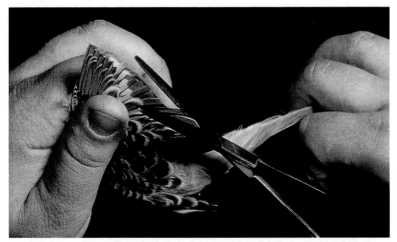

Clipping the wings is essential if you want to let your parakeet out of its cage, but it must be done professionally to prevent problems. Remember that feathers regrow and have to be clipped on a regular basis.

rough or don't hold it properly. A bird has a different way of breathing than we do, and it's possible to prevent it from breathing by holding it around the chest area, even lightly. You should grasp the bird around the neck and the back, leaving the chest free. Your thumb is on one side of the bird's neck, bracing the bottom of its jaw, and your index finger is on the other side, doing the same. The parakeet should look like it's resting with his back in your palm. Of course your parakeet will be struggling, so you can place a washcloth over his feet so he can grasp onto it. A bird that tends to bite can be grasped like this using a thin towel so he can chew on it and not on your fingers.

Once you feel that you're holding your parakeet in the proper fashion, have someone else gently extend its wing and clip the first ten feathers (the long ones at the end of the wing), beginning at the point where the primary feather coverts end—those are the feathers on the upper side of the wing that end at the midpoint of the primary flight feathers. With sharp scissors, clip each feather, one by one, making a clean snip. Clip both wings—if you don't, your parakeet will fly in circles and become flustered and clumsy.

Don't clip your parakeet's wings until you've watched someone do it in person and have had them show you how to hold your bird properly and which feathers to clip. Don't take a pair of sharp scissors to your bird's wings unless you're sure of what you're doing.

Only a properly fed parakeet will have good colors and a perky personality. The best foods help make the best birds.

CHAPTER 6

# *Optimum Nutrition*

An undernourished parakeet is bound to be cranky, feel ill, and will eventually succumb to any number of nutrition-related disorders. Parakeets are not known to be picky eaters, but they do get used to a certain diet readily, and that means that a poor diet can be difficult to change. Feeding your parakeet properly from the very beginning will help to keep it in top shape and keep your veterinary bills low. If you look around a pet shop it might seem that all you have to do is feed your parakeet seeds and change its water—this diet can actually be compared to feeding a prisoner solely bread and water. Not only is an all-seed diet unhealthy, it will barely sustain a parakeet, much less let it thrive.

We know much more about birds and their health needs than we did even fifteen years ago—there's a lot of emphasis placed on good avian nutrition these days, which can make the effort to feed your parakeet properly a little confusing. There are so many different products on the market—seed mixes, pellets, supplements, and treats—where should you begin? This chapter shows you a simple way to feed your parakeet properly and shows you how to get the most nutrition out of the foods you offer.

## STARTING YOUNG

Your baby parakeet is used to eating a certain diet when it comes to you. It's important that you maintain this diet—any sudden change in diet can cause your baby bird to stop eating and become fussy, maybe even ill, or worse. Parakeets are active and have a high metabolism and can lose weight drastically if they don't eat—this is a dangerous situation that can cause seizures and death. Instead of making your parakeet go "cold turkey" on a new, better diet, begin offering new foods gradually and show your bird that they are good by nibbling on them yourself. You can't force a parakeet to gorge on something it doesn't recognize as food, such as a leaf of kale, but if you keep offering it, day after day, the bird will eventually check out the new item. Some owners become frustrated with their birds because the bird refuses a food item for several days. It can take up to two weeks or more for a bird to begin to nibble at a new food, so if you are determined that your parakeet try carrots, keep offering the carrots every day, even if it seems like a waste of time and carrots.

## A NOTE ON CONSISTENCY

Some bird owners become very enthusiastic about their bird's diet for the first few months, making sure that it has the proper amount of everything it needs. Eventually this enthusiasm wanes and the bird is once more on an unbalanced diet, which it quickly gets used to eating. It may be difficult, after a period of time, to get your parakeet to eat properly again, so you want to make sure that you choose to feed a healthy diet that you can maintain. This might mean

**When kept in a pet shop, your parakeet might not have been given the best foods or the cleanest surroundings, so be prepared to improve both conditions at home.**

**Many cages have access doors that allow food to be placed in the cage without chancing that the parakeet will escape.**

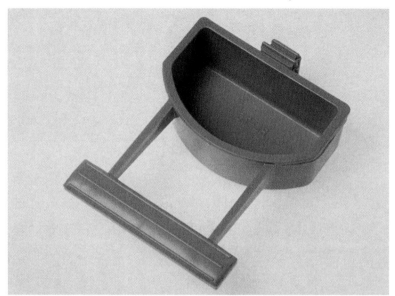

**Feeding dishes should be chosen for ease of cleaning and resistance to chewing by the parakeet.**

preparing foods in advance and keeping them in the freezer or chopping veggies the night before you feed them—but all of this effort is worth it when you realize that you're doing something essential for the health of your parakeet.

## FRESH WATER

Clean, fresh water is essential to your parakeet's well being. You should offer bottled or filtered water only and make sure that you refresh it at least twice a day. Leaving water in the dish too long can cause bacteria to flourish and make your bird ill. Adding a drop or two of apple cider vinegar will help retard the growth of bacteria and is healthful for your bird as well. Supplementing the water with vitamins is not recommended—the vitamins provide bacteria with nutrients for multiplying, turning your bird's water into a slimy mess.

Your parakeet's water dish should be clean enough that you would have no problem drinking from it. You should have two sets of water dishes—one in use and one soaking in a bleach solution and then drying for use the next day. Water bottles not only tend to become clogged, they harbor bacteria in the tube and are more difficult to clean—owners also tend to change the water in them less frequently. Water tubes are also less likely to be changed as often. Instead, use a stainless steel coop cup for water—your parakeet may bathe in it and toss its food inside, but that's what parakeets do— you'll just have to clean it more often. The bonus to that is that your parakeet will always have fresh water.

## THE BASIC DIET

Most people who keep parakeets feed them a diet based on seeds, with the addition of a bounty of fresh foods. An all-seed diet is dead- ly for the parakeet, but a diet that includes seeds can be very bal- anced if you also offer other, more nutritious items. Seed is fatty and doesn't have all the nutrients that your parakeet needs to remain healthy. A parakeet eating only seed will begin to suffer from vari- ous maladies and will eventually die. Seed, in addition to a diet filled with healthy foods, is a fine base diet. You will find seed labeled for parakeets at your pet store—this is the correct mix to feed your para- keet. You can feed a "fancy" expensive mix if you notice that your parakeet enjoys it, but most parakeets will do fine with a plain seed mix. Remember, seeds are not *all* you are going to feed your para- keet—I can't stress that enough.

A good seed mix forms the core of the parakeet's diet but cannot be the only food. Add pellets, vegetables, and fruits for a complete diet.

Keep seeds in an airtight container or in the refrigerator or freezer so that they do not become contaminated with seed flies. Use a clean scoop to dole out the seed instead of dipping your bird's contaminated dish into it.

## A SEED DIET VERSUS A PELLETED DIET

Some manufacturers produce a pelleted diet that consists of small nuggets into which all of the nutrients your parakeet needs are supposedly compacted. Pelleted diets are relatively new on the scene for parrot-type birds, having been used for poultry for many years. The research conducted on poultry nutrition far exceeds the research done on parrot nutrition, and the life of the average pet bird far exceeds that of a chicken. Not much is known on the long-term effects of birds eating these manufactured diets, but there are indications that they can cause liver and kidney damage. Furthermore, a small pellet prepared for a parakeet is also the same pellet prepared for a lovebird and a small conure. How can it be that these very dissimilar birds can thrive on the same formula? Their metabolisms are different and their propensities toward obesity and activity are different as well.

**Some expensive seed mixes contain not only seeds but pellets and nuts. If the items are not too large for your bird, they can be given on occasion but are not necessary.**

## Optimum Nutrition

Some avian experts recommend the use of these diets, suggesting that the bird need only to eat these nuggets and nothing else. For this active, curious parakeet, this is a very boring proposition. Some people feeding pellets as a base diet also include produce and table foods, but this is not recommended according to the pellet manufacturers. This is not to say that you shouldn't feed pellets—they should be a nutritious, fun addition to your parakeet's diet. Offer them in conjunction with all of the other foods you feed—variety in a bird's diet is the key to good health. Pellets are also a great addition to many bird-specific recipes and add a lot of nourishment to the cooked foods you offer your parakeet. Ultimately, your avian veterinarian should be the one to determine the correct diet for your individual bird—if your bird's doctor believes that pellets are the proper base diet, then you should consider making the switch to pellets, though it is your final decision.

### MAKING THE SWITCH TO PELLETS

If your veterinarian advises you to switch to a pelleted diet, you can't simply discontinue seed and expect your parakeet to know that the pellets are food. You might inadvertently starve your parakeet by making it go "cold turkey." Instead, begin mixing the seeds and the pellets at a 50/50 ratio for a week. The next week, mix the seeds at a 40/60 ratio, and so on, until the bowl is filled with only pellets. This may take at least a month. During this time, you should weigh your parakeet on a gram scale to ensure that it is not losing too much weight, and you should carefully watch to make sure that it is actually eating the pellets.

### VEGETABLES AND FRUITS

Vegetables are an important part of your parakeet's diet. Veggies offer a variety of nutrients that your parakeet needs to survive. Fruit is important as well but is full of sugar and can be fattening, though some fruits are so rich in nutrients they are worth the calories! Feed produce that is dark green and orange in color—these items are rich in vitamin A, a nutrient that your parakeet needs for good respiratory health. The following is a list of vegetables and fruits that you can offer every day. Remember, variety is key—offer as many as you can of these items daily:

Yams, (cooked) spinach, pears, broccoli, kale, collard greens, spinach, celery, jalapenos, green pepper, red pepper, yellow pepper, beet tops, pumpkin, zucchini, watercress, peas, corn, green beans, endive, dandelion, asparagus, beets (raw or cooked), carrots (raw or cooked), brussel sprouts, mustard greens, yellow squash, chard, grapes, figs, apples, apricots, watermelon, cantaloupe, bananas, cherries, oranges, peaches, plums, papaya, mango, kiwi, honey dew, berries, grapefruit, and pineapple

Make sure to remove all fruit within a few hours of offering it—it can spoil or attract "fruitflies," pesky little flies that are tough to get rid of. Cooked veggies should also be removed within a few hours if you live in a warm climate.

## TABLE FOODS

Your parakeet can eat just about anything that you eat. The healthier table foods that you can get your parakeet to eat the better. With the exception of chocolate, avocado, rhubarb, alcohol, and salty, sugary, and fatty foods, your bird can eat everything on your plate. Share your meals, and be persistent if your bird is reluctant to try new foods—simply keep offering them and your bird's curiosity will get the best of it. It might seem like cannibalism, but your parakeet might even enjoy a bit of turkey or chicken. Don't forget to bring a "birdy bag" home with you when you go out to eat!

## SNACKS

Many of the commercially available treats are made of seeds. Parakeets that are overfed seeds tend to become obese, especially when they do not get enough exercise. Limit seed treats to once a week—instead, treat your parakeet to a special type of fruit or other healthy snack—this will keep your parakeet from gorging on "candy" and keep his appetite fresh for more nutritious foods. Don't give up on treats though—your parakeet may enjoy the occasional sweet seed stick. Healthy, low-fat snacks include air-popped popcorn, healthy cereal, whole wheat crackers (spread with peanut butter for the occasional sticky treat), and whole wheat bread. Finding out what your parakeet loves is a great training tool. For example, if your bird loves millet spray, use it only during training sessions as a special treat for good behavior.

## FAVORITE FOODS

You will find that your parakeet chooses a couple of favorite foods. This is great if those foods are healthy and nutritious. For example, if your parakeet's favorite foods are kale, carrots, and red peppers, you can feel free to feed them every day. If your bird's favorite foods are millet, celery, and watermelon, you might want to begin limiting those foods and offering more nutritious options—but that does not mean that you have to exclude those favorites forever.

## DIETARY SUPPLEMENTS

Some parakeet owners add supplements to their birds' diet. Common supplements include cuttlebone, mineral block, and calcium powder. Some people drizzle supplemental oils over their birds' seeds and sprinkle supplement powder on top of that. This is not harmful for a parakeet and can even enhance the diet. Consult your veterinarian before you begin to supplement your parakeet's diet. A parakeet that relishes produce, table foods, and pellets and eats a small amount of seed should not require a supplement, though laying hens may need more calcium during breeding season.

The supplement *grit* that you will find in the pet shop is not recommended for parakeets. They do not really need it and may gorge on it and become very ill and even die as a result.

## EXERCISE AND NUTRITION

No discussion of nutrition would be complete without a note on exercise. You know that if you eat a completely healthy diet but do

Calcium often is added to the diet of female parakeets to prevent egg binding. Cuttlebone often is used, but some keepers like to give crushed, boiled eggshell, especially for laying birds.

no exercise, you will not immediately become fit and trim. The same goes for your parakeet. If your parakeet is housed in a large cage or aviary and is allowed to fly, you can be assured that it is getting the exercise it needs—flying is the best form of exercise for a bird. If your parakeet lives in a smallish cage or has its wings clipped, you should make sure that it gets the exercise it needs to remain healthy and fit. This means playing with your parakeet in an active way. You can place it at the bottom of a rope or bird ladder and have it climb up or have it climb from your hand to your shoulder as a game. Even a clipped parakeet enjoys a good wing flapping session and will appreciate being out of the cage so that it can flap away without hitting a toy or the bars of its cage.

## RECIPES FOR YOUR PARAKEET

Cooking food for your parakeet is a great way to provide nutritious, safe, fun foods. Here are a few recipes that you can try. You can freeze portions of each of these and thaw each day for a new, fresh treat. All of these recipes are easy and very variable—you can add whatever you happen to have in the kitchen.

### Bread

Buy a package of corn muffin mix and follow the directions on the package. When you have the batter mixed, add pellets, dried fruit,

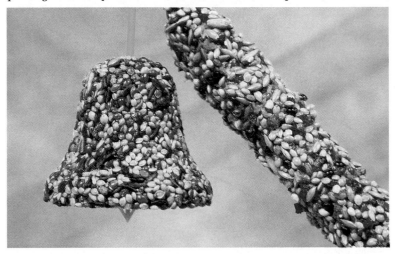

Seeds of various types can be added to many different recipes or even shaped into rods and bells. Try some of the recipes for a bit of easy variety in your parakeet's diet.

**Many parakeets like millet sprays both as a food and as a toy.**

canned beans (any kind), broccoli (or other veggie), 2 tbsp of crushed cuttlebone, 2 tbsp chunky peanut butter, and anything else you think your parakeet might like. Bake until a knife comes out clean from the center of the bread—this may take far longer than the package recommends.

### Pancakes

Make pancake batter the way you normally would (if you're like me, use instant), and add pellets, dried apricots, and shredded carrots. Make like regular pancakes. You can add anything else to the batter you think your parakeet might like.

### Omelet

Crack several eggs into a bowl, including the shells, and add pellets, two types of chopped veggies, dried fruit, and anything else your parakeet will like. Cook as an omelet or scramble. Cook extremely well—chicken eggs can pass on disease to parrot-type birds. Freeze and thaw a small portion each day.

### Pasta

Boil whole wheat pasta and drain. Pour it in a saucepan and melt soy cheese over it. Add pellets, veggies, bananas, crushed hard-boiled egg (including shell), or whatever else your parakeet likes. You can freeze this in ice cube trays and defrost a cube a day. Makes a nutritious and colorful treat!

PARAKEETS

A properly trained parakeet is a great household pet that can be enjoyed by all the family members.

# CHAPTER 7

# *Parakeet Behavior*

Birds are often difficult to understand—it sometimes seems that they come from another planet. This is likely due to the fact that our companion birds, including the parakeet, are not domestic animals, even though parakeets have been kept in captivity for many years. A domestic animal is one that humans have changed through selective breeding to suit our needs. The cow, for example, can be bred to have a certain fat content in its flesh or to produce milk with certain desired components. Dogs are bred to accomplish certain tasks, such as herding or hunting vermin—their instincts are selected and honed by breeders. Companion birds, on the other hand, have not been changed so drastically that they have lost their natural instincts. We can understand why a Border Collie herds sheep, but we have a difficult time understanding why our parakeets want to chew the wallpaper—this behavior seems to serve no purpose.

The parakeet is an animal that acts out of pure instinct. It does not do things to spite you, nor does it do things to assist you—it merely acts out of a desire to fulfill its natural urges, whether that be chewing, chattering, or cuddling. The parakeet, in general, is a lively creature that is at once loyal and territorial, and its normal behaviors can often seem bewildering to an owner who is not used to observing this special little pet. This chapter will help to take some of the confusion out of why parakeets behave the way they do.

## PARAKEET INTELLIGENCE

The parakeet is a bright bird, able to learn to do things all on its own, like open its cage door to escape or make a racket for attention. Do not underestimate the intelligence of this bird—it might be a bird but it's no birdbrain! The parakeet will learn things all on its own,

Parakeets that have been raised with other birds and are not fully socialized may be difficult to train, but almost any parakeet will eventually be trainable.

but can be stubborn about learning things you want to teach it, though most parakeets are highly trainable. The "inability" to learn a behavior or trick does not mean that your parakeet is a stupid bird, but that it's a highly self-directed animal or, perhaps, that you are not teaching it correctly or with the proper amount of patience. The key to training your parakeet is to understand your bird's limitations and to appreciate it as an individual. Luckily for the parakeet owner, this species, although as independent as any companion bird, is easily trained with gentle, repetitive methods and patience.

## VOCALIZATION

The longer you live with a parakeet the more you will notice that your bird has many different styles of vocalization. Parakeets will even vocalize differently at certain times of the day. Most owners are curious about what these vocalizations mean. Birds do indeed have their own language. Again, what they are "saying" has to do with their needs. For example, if there's danger around, say your parakeet notices something frightening in its environment, it will vocalize in a shrill, loud, and insistent voice. This is to alert the other members of the flock (your family) about the danger, even if the "danger" is just a mouse scurrying along the floor. Of course, parakeets have actually alerted their human flock to such dangers as burglars and gas leaks. Parakeets make conscientious pets.

Normal vocalization occurs in different forms throughout the day. When the sun rises your parakeet might greet the dawn with chirping. This is the time when it would be calling to the other members of the flock to let them know it made it through the night.

Throughout the day your parakeet will alternate between periods of silence and singing, chirping, and talking (or chattering).

It's an uncanny thing to see your parakeet fast asleep and singing away as if he were awake. A parakeet taking a little "cat nap" throughout the daylight hours will chirp and bob its head and tail as he sleeps. This is to give a predator the illusion that it's still alert and awake. This is called sleeping vocalizations.

A parakeet will repeat his dawn vocalizations at dusk. This is "all's well" chatter.

Parakeets won't vocalize during the night, unless you leave the lights or television on. A wild parakeet vocalizing in the night would

**Starting bonding and training early is the best bet, which is why hand-raised parakeets make the best pets.**

be a great target for predators. Don't worry about being awakened by your parakeet—it will sleep until the sun rises or until you uncover his cage. If you hear vocalization at night, be sure to check out your parakeet's cage—something might be wrong.

If you want to sleep late, make it a habit of covering your parakeet's cage at night and taking the cover off when *you* want to wake up. This is a perfectly fine way to control your parakeet's vocalizations. It's not fine, however, to keep a parakeet covered for most of the day—your parakeet needs at least eight to ten hours of "daylight" and interaction with the world for each 24-hour period.

Parakeets also vocalize to maintain contact with their flockmates— in this case, that means you. If your parakeet is very bonded to you, he will call you constantly, waiting for you to answer. When you don't come or answer him, he will call again and again, until you do. A simple way to get him to stop calling you *to a degree* is to call back to him, telling him you're okay and that you're in the kitchen, etc. This way he'll be reassured that his flock is accounted for and he may be quiet for a little while—until he decides that he wants to know where you are again.

**Parakeets are vocal birds, so they whistle and chatter much of the day, especially when a pair spends lots of time calling to each other.**

*Parakeet Behavior*

**Vocalizations are most common at dawn and dusk but continue through the day as "contact notes"—sort of "I'm here, where are you?"**

If you have a pair or more of parakeets, chances are that they will be calling one another throughout the day. The more parakeets you have, the noisier your home will be. The good news is that the parakeet's voice is pleasant and not as loud as some other members of the parrot family. Many parakeet owners actually love the constant chatter, even when they have dozens of birds chattering away at the same time.

## BODY LANGUAGE

You can tell a lot about a how parakeet feels by its body language. Close observation of your parakeet may reveal the following body language:

*Sleeping on one foot:* This means that the parakeet is healthy and content. A parakeet sleeping on two feet may not be feeling well or may be too warm.

*Feather fluffing:* A quick ruffle of the feathers signifies a content bird that is releasing tension and getting ready to perform another task, such as flying or moving to the water dish. A parakeet that is sitting on a perch with its feathers fluffed may not be feeling well or might be cold. If your parakeet is fluffed, backed into a corner, wings shaking, and beak open, it's displaying territorial behavior—watch your fingers—this is a bird that's going to bite!

*Stretching:* Parakeets stretch for the same reasons we do—because it feels good, to release tension, and to get tired muscles moving again.

*Yawning:* Birds yawn to clear their nasal passages, just like we do. If you notice excessive yawning in your parakeet, it might indicate a health problem. Never try to remove anything from your bird's nose.

*Tail bobbing:* A singing or chirping parakeet will have a wildly bobbing tail. If your parakeet's tail is bobbing a lot while it's resting on a perch, it could indicate a respiratory problem.

*Elimination posture:* A parakeet that's about to eliminate will back up a little, wag its tail, and then bombs away! Get to know this posture if you want to avoid having to change your T-shirt!

## NORMAL BEHAVIORS

Parakeets can do some pretty uncanny things that will look like problem behaviors, when they are actually quite healthy and normal. Look for these normal behaviors in your parakeet:

*Preening:* Preening is when your parakeet runs its beak through its feathers, making sure they are all clean and in place. Each

### Parakeet Behavior

feather is made up of little strands that zip together like Velcro—your parakeet spends a lot of time making sure that each feather is zipped properly. Preening isn't just for vanity purposes. It keeps the feathers clean for flying and for insulation.

*Beak grinding:* When a parakeet is sleepy and content it will audibly grind the two parts of its beak together. Experts cannot find a distinct reason for this—parakeets seem to do it simply because they want to.

*Beak wiping:* When a parakeet eats a particularly juicy or messy meal, it will wipe its beak along the sides of its cage or on a perch, usually the concrete conditioning perch, if one is provided. This is akin to a human wiping her face with a napkin and is one reason why it's a good idea to disinfect and scrub perches weekly.

*Wing flapping:* Wing flapping while standing on a perch provides much needed exercise for a clipped bird. A bird that's flapping its wings might be testing out newly grown-in feathers. Wing waving while chirping is a sign of a content, happy bird that's calling out to communicate with other birds or its owner.

*Door dancing:* A parakeet that is allowed frequent out-of-cage time might develop a little door-dance—it will stand in front of its

**Wiping the beak on a branch is a natural way of removing food particles and juices, and pets often will do this in their cages.**

PARAKEETS **91**

cage door and move back and forth, clambering around, desperately trying to get your attention. This is a sign that your parakeet is well bonded to you.

*Flattened posture, wings shaking:* This posture means that your parakeet desperately wants something or wants to go somewhere— it is ready to take action on its desire, which may mean launching itself toward the object it wants.

*Regurgitation:* As unpleasant as it sounds, a parakeet that is bobbing its head in your direction may be "affectionately" regurgitating to you. This is a high compliment. Rarely will a parakeet actually vomit *on* you, making a mess—it's more the thought that counts in this case. Male parakeets are more likely to do this than females, so don't get offended if your female parakeet doesn't show this behavior.

*Head down:* A parakeet that is very bonded to you might desire a bit of head and neck scratching and will show you this by putting its head down for you and offering you a fluffed neck. Gently rub your bird against the feathers and circle the ear openings lightly—this may cause your parakeet to yawn—then you know you're doing it right!

*Chewing:* Parakeets love to chew. This is a normal behavior. Don't take it as an aggressive act if your parakeet chews your signed Picasso to bits—it's just doing what its instincts tell it to do. If you want to save your priceless antiques, provide your bird with plenty of things to chew, including store-bought toys and household items, such as toilet paper rolls (but make sure your parakeet's head doesn't become stuck in one).

## PROBLEM BEHAVIORS

Because parakeets are not domestic animals and their life in a home is truly a foreign experience, your pet parakeet may acquire problem behaviors that can cause some concern in an owner who doesn't understand why the behaviors are happening nor how to change them. Here are a few of the common behavior issues that parakeets face.

*Biting:* A parakeet's beak, though not large, is very sharp and can cause bleeding to the sensitive skin on human fingers. One way to prevent biting is to play with your parakeet every day and keep it tame. If your once-tame parakeet is already biting, one way to *keep* it biting is to show fear and retreat every time it gnashes its beak at you. This retreat will teach the parakeet that it is more powerful than you and that biting is a great way to get you to leave it alone. To disarm a biting parakeet, move its cage to another room before you take it out or gather it up in a towel and take the bird to a different location. This will distract the bird and allow you to play with it without being bitten. Once the bird sees that playing with you is fun and that you're not afraid of it, the biting may cease, though this may take several weeks. Giving a biting parakeet a "time out," just as you would a child having a tantrum, is a good way to teach it that biting is not going to be tolerated. Simply remove the biting bird to a small "time out" cage placed in a quiet corner—this cage shouldn't have toys or treats in it. When the bird is in this cage you will not interact with it, but wait for it to calm down and compose itself. This is often an effective method of quelling biting—the worst punishment for a bird is to ignore it. Leave it in the time out cage for no more than five to ten minutes, at most. Never, ever hit a bird or flick or strike the beak in any way—a bird's beak is very sensitive and flicking it with a fingernail can really hurt and your bird will begin to mistrust you. You can hold the upper part of a parakeet's beak slightly if it persists in biting; say "no!" firmly (don't yell), though most parakeets will continue doing what they want to do anyway. A parakeet that continues biting may not be feeling well—look for signs of illness and take your bird to the veterinarian if you suspect something is wrong.

*The jewel thief:* Parakeets adore shiny objects and will quickly abscond with an earring—right out of your ear! It can also break a gold chain and make off with the pendants. This is normal, though annoying behavior and can be prevented by removing jewelry before playing with the bird.

*Self-mutilation:* When a parakeet is bored, confined, mistreated, has nutritional deficiencies, or has experienced a drastic change in its life, it may begin to pick out its feathers or chew other parts of its body, resulting in bleeding and bald patches. This is a terrible state for a parakeet, who uses self-mutilation as a last resort to distract itself from deplorable living circumstances. Sometimes a parakeet that has an illness, such as a problem with its respiratory system, will pluck the feathers around the area that disturbs it. Plucking and other mutilating behaviors always need medical attention. To prevent boredom plucking, provide your parakeet with a spacious cage and lots of different types of toys to chew and play with.

*Persistent vocalizations:* A parakeet can be persistently noisy, especially if it knows that its owner will come running every time it kicks up a racket. There is a difference between a parakeet that's

Even a young parakeet will bite when picked up, at least until it learns what is going on, and its beak is its major defensive weapon. Early socialization prevents biting when the bird is older and the bite more painful.

vocalizing normally and one that's vocalizing to get attention. Of course, you want to give your parakeet as much attention as possible, but there will be times when you will want your bird to play independently, without expecting to be on your shoulder all day. A dark cage cover works well to quiet a noisy parakeet, but it should not be used during the day for more than ten minutes at a time. But a cover only treats the problem, not the root of the problem. Try to find out why your parakeet is screaming or vocalizing loudly. Perhaps something is frightening it. Perhaps you've inadvertently trained it to scream every time you leave the room by reinforcing the behavior by returning to the cage and talking to or playing with the bird. Look at your actions and see if the persistent noise is a result of something you've been doing.

*Egg laying in the single hen:* Egg laying can pose a health and behavior problem in female parakeets. She may become depleted of calcium from laying eggs to replace the ones you remove and she can become territorial of her "nest." To prevent her from laying eggs, remove anything that she might consider a nesting site and decrease the availability of bright light to eight or nine hours a day—this will lead her to believe that it's not breeding season. If this fails, try moving the cage to another location. Males also tend to become aggressive and will mate with their toys if they feel that it's time to breed. Use the same methods described above to keep your male parakeet's hormones in check.

To train your parakeet, you must have a relationship with your bird. Parakeets bond to humans and treat them like other parakeets.

C H A P T E R    8

# Relationship Based Taming and Training

If you have a single parakeet, chances are that you will want it to be tame and come out of its cage to cuddle and play with you. Once a parakeet is bonded to a person it is quite loyal and shows a deep affection for its owner. Training a parakeet to be tame and playful is easy. This outgoing and sociable bird takes well to life in the average home.

Parakeets are indeed trainable to perform certain simple behaviors, and they are even known to be good at "tricks." However, it is actually more likely that your parakeet will train you than the other way around. Your parakeet will teach you to do its bidding quickly. Parakeets are fast learners. If your parakeet is begging to be let out of its cage with high-pitched whistles and a frantic dance in front of its door and you open the cage, it will soon learn that this method works. If you don't mind this behavior, you can continue reinforcing it by giving in to your bird; if not, ignoring the behavior is the first step in stopping it.

For optimal training, you must develop a relationship with your parakeet. This means that you will not force it to do anything it doesn't want to do and that you respect it as you would a good friend. A bird that views its owner as a friend is more likely to do what its owner wants it to do. In other words, fear tactics don't work with birds; gentle, patient training methods do. Make a friend of your parakeet from the very beginning. Talk softly to it and handle it tenderly. Come to know it as an individual. Just as some humans are smarter than others or are more apt to learn certain things, so too with the parakeet. Know your parakeet's limitations before you set out to teach it complicated behaviors. Having a great relationship with your parakeet, one that's based on mutual give and take,

P A R A K E E T S                                                           **97**

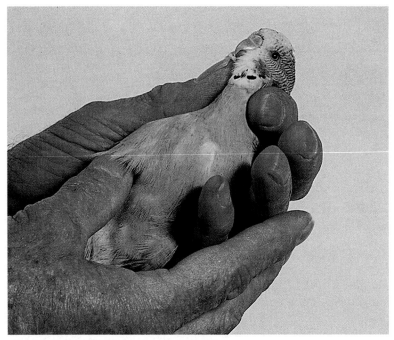

**The proper way to hold a parakeet for examination or grooming.**

is better than forcing an unwilling bird to do something it's not meant to do.

## HOUSEHOLD RULES

Teaching your parakeet household rules is like teaching a two-year-old child the same—it can be done using a lot of repetition. However, some rules may never be learned, which is why parakeets need supervision when they are out of the cage. Parakeet-proofing your home, making it a safe place for your parakeet to play, will help in preventing mischief and tragedy.

Create household rules for every human member of the family who interacts with the parakeet. One member may try to train a certain behavior; another will try to teach it something different; still another may be treating the bird with impatience. Agreeing on how the parakeet will be handled goes a long way toward proper training. Some trainers will suggest that only one person train the bird. This is ideal, but it is hardly realistic, especially if there are children involved. Everyone in the household can participate in training the bird, as long as there are "ground rules" to how and what the bird is learning.

Children, in particular, must be "trained" to handle the parakeet with composure and decorum. Teach children how to treat the new bird gently and calmly from the very beginning, and supervise all young children while they are handling the bird.

## TRAINING A YOUNG PARAKEET

A very young parakeet is easy to handle. It has not yet learned to bite and will be more apt to be gentle and willing to try new things. Handle your parakeet every day. Cuddle and play with it. When it begins to nip at your hands or your neck, even if the bird is just playing, you must stop it from nibbling and tell it "no!" in a firm voice. Little nibbles from a youngster will turn into hard biting when the bird gets a little older. Preventing bad behavior in a youngster will avoid you having to train the behavior out of it once the bird gets older. It is far easier to train a good behavior *into* a bird than it is to stop a bird from doing something it has gotten used to. Using the "no!" command is generally effective in stopping a behavior at the

**Start training a parakeet as young as possible. Babies are easier to handle, more docile, and bond quickly.**

moment, but the bird often goes right back to doing what it wants to do. Keeping a close eye on your parakeet will help to prevent mischief and trouble.

## TAMING THE SEMI-TAME PARAKEET

A semi-tame parakeet is one that has experience with humans but is not all that trustful of them. This bird can be tamed easily if you take some simple steps toward developing a trusting relationship with it. There are two ways to tame a parakeet: you can "break" it or you can "gentle" it. Using a gentle, slow training method is always preferable with animals as sensitive as parakeets. "Breaking" a parakeet, using quick, violent training, will work for a time but will not allow a real bond to form between you and your parakeet. Your parakeet will always be wary of you, and birds have excellent memories.

When you first bring your semi-tame parakeet home you will want to give it a period of adjustment. Your bird will be stressed in its new situation and may even flap around the cage when you approach. Do not consider taming it until it has settled into a routine. This may

**Most pet shop parakeets are semi-tame, used to humans but not really bonded. Your job as a trainer will be to increase the bond with your bird through slow and gentle training.**

Some parakeets that are not used to humans may be fearful of people and hard to train. They may bite, stay at the back of their cage, and not cooperate. With time, even these birds may be trained.

take a few days to a couple of weeks. Once a parakeet is eating well, vocalizing, preening, and bathing, it is adjusted to its new home.

Once the parakeet is settled in, you can begin taming. You will first need to clip the bird's wings. A parakeet allowed free flight will simply fly away from you and not return. Even if you eventually want to allow your bird to fly, you will have to clip the wings during the training period—the feathers will grow back in time.

Once the bird's wings are clipped you can begin the taming process. If your bird is untamed or semi-tame, fish it out of its cage with a small towel and hold it gently in the towel to prevent it from biting you. It may scream and struggle, but continue to be calm and talk to it in a low, soothing voice. Take the bird to a small room—a bathroom is ideal, but be sure to close the toilet lid and remove any dangerous items that may fall and break if the bird comes in contact with them. Sit on the floor with your knees bent and place the bird gently on top of your knee, holding it there for a moment before you let go. The moment you let go, the bird will probably flutter away from you in an escape attempt. Gather up the bird again and try to place it on your knee again. Repeat this action until the bird eventually stands on your knee for a moment. Remember to remain calm. The bird may not want to stand on your knee in the first few sessions, but keep trying. You can do this twice a day for 20 minutes each session, but no more than that. You want to begin to build trust between you and the bird, not stress it out.

Once you've gotten your bird to stand on your knee, talk to it in a very calm voice and begin to move one hand slowly up your leg toward the bird. This may cause it to flutter off of your knee again. No matter—simply try again. Little by little, session after session, move your hand slowly up your leg until the bird allows it to come very close. The idea here is that the bird should eventually allow contact with your hand. This may take quite a while, so be patient. Once the bird allows your hand to approach closely, try to tickle its chest with your finger or scratch its head and neck if it allows, still moving very slowly. After a few sessions, you can try to get the bird to stand on your hand. Remember, all of this should be done with a lot of patience.

At the end of the training session, place your parakeet back in its cage—if you have trouble doing this, put your hand gently over the bird's back—this way it can't open its wings to try to fly away or attempt to climb on the cage. Give it a treat and tell it how good a bird it was. After a few moments you can allow it out for independent playtime.

**Train your parakeet to get on a stick as early as possible. This will make it easier to capture escapees without resorting to a net or other stressful methods.**

If your bird is young and not a biter, you can simply place the bird on your finger and sit in a small, safe room with it, talking to it in a low, soothing voice. Put it on your shoulder while you watch television or while you eat, offering it healthy food from your meal. The bird will soon realize that it's fun to interact with you.

## DISCIPLINE

Proper discipline for a bird consists of one method—ignoring it. This is the worst punishment for a bird. It will learn very quickly that it doesn't get to play if it bites or screams. Placing a biting bird in a time-out cage for a few minutes is a good way to show it that you're not thrilled with its behavior. After a particularly unwanted behavior, you can ignore your bird for up to ten minutes. Don't ignore the bird for long periods of time because that can be very stressful for this flock-oriented animal.

There are a few things you should never do to your parakeet during training or at any other time. This improper discipline will only result in breaking the trust that you and your parakeet need to build in order to have a mutually satisfying relationship.

Never hit, flick, squeeze, or throw your parakeet. This is animal abuse and will make your parakeet mistrust you.

Never throw anything at your parakeet's cage to make it stop vocalizing. Throwing things at the cage will make your parakeet feel very insecure.

Never "play rough" with your parakeet. This will teach it to be aggressive and to bite.

Never cover the cage for long periods during the day. If you have a sleeping infant or you simply need your bird to quiet down, you can cover the cage for an hour or so, but it's cruel to cover it for extended periods when your parakeet should be active.

Never starve your parakeet as a training tool. Sure, your bird will be hungry and might do what you want it to do for a seed, but this might backfire on you and cause your bird to become ill. Parakeets have high metabolisms and can have seizures and even die if their blood sugar drops too low.

## TEACHING THE STEP-UP COMMAND

Of all the behaviors you can teach your parakeet, the step-up command is possibly the most important. This command allows you to retrieve your parakeet at any time and is especially useful when it is behaving fussy or is in potential danger. Step-up is when your parakeet

A cage cover can be used at night for darkness and security, and can be used to give the bird a very short "time out."

steps gently on to your hand or finger without hesitation. A parakeet is not hatched knowing how to do this, so you must teach it. Perhaps your parakeet came to you already tame and hand trained—that's great! But it's still important to reinforce the step-up command so that it becomes second nature to you and to your parakeet.

Assuming that you are teaching a tame or semi-tame parakeet the step-up command, begin by allowing the parakeet to come out of its cage on its own. You win nothing by fishing the parakeet out violently and will only succeed in beginning your training session on a bad note. Place a perch on top of its cage or let the bird climb on to a standing perch where it will be standing on a round dowel, not a flat surface. If your parakeet is a youngster, you can gently lift it out of the cage, but since it doesn't yet know how to step up, be careful not to pull too hard on its feet—it will grip the perch, not understanding what you want.

Once the parakeet is out, give it a treat, either a bit of yummy food or a good head scratching. This will show the bird that training sessions can be fun, and it will look forward to them. Next, begin rubbing your bird's chest and belly very softly and gently with the length of your index finger, cooing to him, slowly increasing the pressure with which you push on its chest. You may have to repeat this for a few days, depending on the tameness of your parakeet. Your semi-tame parakeet may not be sure what you are up to and might be wary of this attention. Take things slowly and work to gain its trust. A tamer parakeet will often sit quietly, enjoying the attention.

Once you feel that your parakeet is calm and used to this process, you can increase the pressure you place on its chest. Pushing slightly on a parakeet's chest will throw it off balance, and it will lift up a foot to right itself. Place your finger or hand under the foot and lift him, if it allows it. If not, simply allow its foot to remain on your hand until the bird removes it. As you do this, tell your bird clearly to "step-up." You must always say "step-up" when it steps on to your hand—it is key that your parakeet associates the action of stepping onto your hand with the phrase.

Once your parakeet is fairly good at stepping up, you can have it step from finger to finger, repeating the phrase "step-up" and praising it. Your bird may hesitate at first, but soon it will know exactly what you want. Be sure that your training sessions last only a few minutes each, and try not to become frustrated if your parakeet doesn't do exactly what you want right away. Training sessions are ideally short,

**By using the "step-up" command, you can easily train your parakeet to walk onto the end of a stick. You'll appreciate this when you have to get your bird down off the drapes.**

perhaps ten to fifteen minutes twice a day, and should be incorporated into playtime.

Most youngsters will learn the step-up command easily, in one or two short sessions, while a semi-tame parakeet may take longer— the more your parakeet trusts you, the easier it will be to teach it. Remember, patience is key. Even if this command is the only "trick" you teach your parakeet, it is by far the most valuable. If you make sure to say "step-up" every time you lift your parakeet, you will reinforce this important training every day and will make life much easier for both of you.

## STICK TRAINING

Stick training is simply teaching the "step-up" command using a perch or dowel instead of your finger. It is very important that your parakeet know how to step onto a stick. The day may come when your parakeet refuses to come down from the curtain rod or gets out of the house and is sitting high in a tree, chirping away. A parakeet that has been stick trained will be easy to retrieve with a long dowel or broomstick. A parakeet that is not used to stepping onto a stick will be terrified of it and you may lose the opportunity to save your bird from harm. Teach "step-up" with a stick the same way you teach it with your finger. Stick training should begin as soon as you begin hand taming your parakeet. If your bird is terrified of the stick, you can leave it close to the cage where your bird will have a chance to view it and get used to its presence. Use different types of sticks during training so that your parakeet learns not to be afraid of various dowels and perches.

## TAMING THE BRONCO PARAKEET

The bronco parakeet is one that has not had much, if any, handling by humans. It is generally fearful of humans and can be aggressive but is not impossible to tame. The first thing you have to do with the bronco, after letting it adjust to its new home, is show it that you are not afraid of it. The bronco bird will want nothing more than to be left alone and will show you this by biting. If you are bitten and you retreat, you show the bird that it has the upper hand. The best way to deal with biting is to avoid being bitten. This means that you may want to work with stick training before you begin using your hands. Putting on thick gloves will only frighten your parakeet more and hinder training, so don't use them.

*Relationship Based Taming and Training*

Being afraid of your parakeet's beak is an understandable fear, especially when the bird is untamed. If this is the case, try the "whittle down" method. Begin by stick training your bird with the step-up command using a 12- to 18-inch dowel or perch—use a width sized appropriately for a parakeet. Once your bird learns to step on to the stick and does it with ease, begin cutting the stick down, about an inch each week, until the stick is very short. Eventually, if you've done this slowly enough and have worked to gain your bird's trust, the stick will be so short that your parakeet will step onto your hand.

If your parakeet is really wild, you can use the towel method for the first few training sessions. Hold the bird properly and gently in a towel and talk softly to it while caressing its head. Do this twice a day for the first few days before you begin training in the bathroom. This will show your parakeet that you are not to be feared and that you mean no harm. Use this method *only* if you are certain that holding your parakeet is not causing it pain or undue stress, and do it only for a few minutes at a time.

## TEACHING YOUR PARAKEET TO TALK

Parakeets are among the absolute best talkers in the parrot family, able to learn hundreds of words and phrases. Many owners take delight in their parakeet's vocabulary—indeed this is one aspect that makes parakeet ownership popular.

Teaching your parakeet to talk is pretty easy but it can take some time. Some gifted parakeets will learn to talk in just a few weeks, while others may not talk for a year. Patience and repetition are key.

The first attempts at talking will sound like garbled English. This is "baby talk"—once baby talk begins, you'll start to hear the words become clearer. This is the time to correct your bird's pronunciation, repeating the phrases that it's attempting (if you understand them) back to it, the way they should sound. You'll be surprised at how clearly your parakeet will begin to repeat the words if you teach it how they're meant to be said.

Pairs will be less likely to talk than the single bird, and single birds with mirrors will be less likely to talk than single birds without mirrors—if a parakeet has something to talk to, it won't talk to you. It is sad to have a bird be lonely to become a talker—perhaps you can compromise. Wait until your bird learns to talk well *then* get it a friend to pal around with.

A parakeet learning to talk is its way of learning your language, of trying to communicate with you. Talking indicates a deep affection

A parakeet that is aloof may be difficult to train, as it is not bonding well with you. Use the most gentle methods for training and be prepared to spend a long time working with the bird, but you will eventually succeed.

(or at least a heightened attentiveness) for a parakeet's owners. The more attention and affection you lavish on your parakeet, the more likely it is to talk to you.

Male parakeets speak more frequently and will learn more words than females—this is just one of those facts of parakeet life. There are exceptions, but this is the general rule for talking parakeets. Hens do become capable whistlers, however, so don't fret if you have a female.

If you want your parakeet to talk, don't teach it to whistle first. Whistling is easier and more fun, apparently, than talking and is often preferred. You can teach your bird to excel at whistling after he has learned several phrases. Of course, if you have a hen, you might want to just teach whistling from the beginning.

The only way to teach your parakeet to talk is to repeat yourself—a lot. A parakeet has to hear a word or phrase over and over many times before it masters it. Once you've decided on a phrase you want your parakeet to learn, say it over and over every time you pass the cage, and be sure to say it clearly so that your bird will hear it correctly.

## TRICK TRAINING

Parakeets can be taught simple tricks, but they are not known to be highly proficient at learning intricate behaviors, the way a larger bird might. Perhaps it's just that they are reluctant learners. Whatever the case, you might become frustrated trying to teach your parakeet complicated tricks.

The best way to teach your parakeet tricks is to capitalize on its natural behavior. For example, if you notice that your parakeet is wonderful at climbing, place it on the end of a long piece of rope and encourage it to climb up, praising it in a high-pitched voice when it completes the task. Remember, whenever you want to teach your parakeet anything, use a lot of praise and make the training session fun. Also, if you can find a treat that your parakeet adores, millet spray, for example, use it in your training sessions rather than just offering it freely in the cage.

Keeping your parakeet healthy is more than a matter of medicines and vet visits. It also involves providing proper care, good cages, and nonstressing surroundings.

CHAPTER 9

# *Beyond Good Health*

Even though parakeets are small, inexpensive birds, they still need proper veterinary care and an owner who is responsible and willing to provide it. Often, people think of parakeets as "lesser" pets, easily replaceable, not worthy of an expensive trip to the veterinarian. This is not a great way to perceive a pet, one that will outlive the family dog if given the proper care.

## GROOMING FOR HEALTH

Grooming your bird is one step you can take to keep it healthy and safe. Grooming a bird includes clipping the flight feathers, keeping the toenails trimmed, and making sure that the beak is properly aligned and isn't growing too long.

If you play with your parakeet regularly you might notice that its toenails pinch and prick you uncomfortably. This is the time to trim its toenails. If your parakeet has a conditioning perch made of concrete or another rough material, you may only have to trim the toenails three or four times a year. Your parakeet's toenails should have a graceful half-moon curve to them—if they extend beyond this, your bird might have a medical problem related to a nutritional deficiency or could potentially have mites. See your veterinarian if your parakeet's toenails seem unusual in any way.

A bird's toenails are like our toenails—there's a dead part and a living part, called the quick. When trimming your bird's nails you only want to cut off the dead part of the nail. Cutting into the quick is very painful and causes bleeding. Trim the nails conservatively. In a bird with clear or pink nails, it will be easy to see the quick and avoid cutting into it. In a bird with dark nails you will only want to take off the very tip of the nail. You can use a small nail clipper to trim the nails, which may be a two-person job—one to hold the bird properly and one to trim the nails. If bleeding does occur, simply apply styptic power to the wound and the bleeding should stop.

There should never be a reason for you to groom your parakeet's beak. Eating hard items, chewing toys, and rubbing its beak on a conditioning perch will all help to keep the bird's beak trimmed and properly aligned. In some cases, when a parakeet is ill or has a severe nutritional deficiency or mites, the beak may become elongated and may interfere with eating. This is a case for a veterinarian's treatment. You can severely injure your parakeet by trying to trim the beak yourself.

## MOLTING

When birds molt they shed their feathers and make way for new ones to grow. The old feathers may have become ragged and not useful for insulation or flying anymore. A molt can happen once or twice a year, depending on the amount of light and warmth your parakeet is exposed to, and it is a very stressful time for a bird. Your parakeet may become ill-tempered and not want to be touched at certain times. The newly growing feathers can be uncomfortable or tender. You will notice little "pins" beginning to poke out from between your parakeet's other feathers. These are called pin feathers. The "pin" is a sheath of material (keratin) that protects the new feather until it is ready to emerge. Your parakeet will spend time removing these sheathes, but will not be able to remove the ones on its head—if your bird allows head scratching, you can gently remove them just as a its mate would.

Molting birds do not lose all of their feathers at once. Most molts are many weeks or months long, and feathers are replaced gradually. If you notice bald patches on your parakeet's body or its feathers become so thin you can see the skin beneath them, take your bird to your avian veterinarian right away—there may be a serious problem.

Pin feathers and new feathers that have just emerged from the sheath have a blood supply and will bleed if injured or broken, which can happen easily with parakeets that experience night thrashing. Breakage often happens with a wing feather, especially in a clipped bird, who does not have fully grown wing feathers that would protect a new feather from breaking. If you notice a bleeding feather, perhaps one that was clipped during wing trimming, don't panic. Pull the feather straight out from the root with one quick

Parakeets lose their feathers slowly, one or two at a time, over a period of several weeks, replacing them with new feathers growing near the bases of the old feathers. Molts occur once or twice a year.

motion and the bleeding will stop immediately. A pair of needle-nosed pliers is good for this purpose and should be kept in your bird first aid kit. If you're squeamish about this, apply styptic powder to the bleeding area and take your bird to your avian veterinarian as soon as possible.

Regular misting with warm water is helpful in softening the pin feathers. Only mist your bird in temperate weather and when there's adequate time for it to dry before evening. Offer your parakeet an extra-nutritious diet during molting, including a protein source, such as hardboiled eggs, egg food, and boiled chicken. You shouldn't notice any difference in the way your parakeet behaves, eats, plays, or responds to you during a molt, but there is the possibility for it to behave differently while the new feathers are emerging.

## BATHING YOUR PARAKEET

If you offer your parakeet water in a coop cup it will bathe itself, splashing water all over the cage and surrounding area. Some very tame parakeets will enjoy bathing in a soft stream of water coming from the kitchen sink's tap or will even enjoy sitting on a special perch while their owner is showering. A mister simulating rain is a good way to get your parakeet to bathe. Bathing is important for your parakeet not only because it keeps the bird clean, but because it encourages preening. You bird only needs clean, fresh water for bathing. There are bathing products that you can buy from the pet shop, but they are not really necessary. Bathe your bird only in warm weather and in the daytime, allowing plenty of time for it to dry thoroughly. Never use soaps or other detergents.

## KEEPING YOUR PARAKEET HEALTHY

Once you acquire your new parakeet, you should make an appointment in the first three days to see an avian veterinarian near you. An avian veterinarian is a doctor who has been trained to treat the illnesses and injuries of birds. The avian veterinarian has experience with recognizing and treating illnesses particular to birds, whose bodily systems are far different from those of a dog or cat. Your avian veterinarian is your first line of defense in keeping your parakeet healthy. A "well-bird" check up will ensure that your bird is healthy and will begin a relationship with the doctor that will last the lifetime of your bird. Many veterinarians will not treat emergencies unless the patient is already registered at the

*Beyond Good Health*

office, so you might find yourself in a dire situation if you haven't created this valuable relationship.

Take your parakeet to the avian veterinarian at least once a year. This will enable the doctor to weigh the bird and to perform routine tests that will show any changes and indicate any potential disorders. This is also a good time to discuss your bird's diet and have the doctor trim its nails.

Choosing an avian veterinarian takes a bit more effort than just finding one near your home. Make sure that the doctor has a good bedside manner and is open to your questions and concerns. Ask the veterinarian if she has birds of her own. Find out what hours the office is open and what the emergency treatment policy is. Find an avian veterinarian that will speak to you in the middle of the night should your bird become injured. When you visit the office, look around to make sure that it's clean and talk to the staff to see if they are friendly and efficient.

You can locate an avian veterinarian by calling the Association of Avian Veterinarians at: (561) 393-9801 or going to their site on the Internet at www.aav.com. The American Federation of Aviculture can be contacted at: (602) 484-0931 or on the web at www.afa.birds.org. The American Federation of Aviculture also has information on how to find an avian veterinarian in your area.

## SIGNS AND SYMPTOMS OF AN ILL PARAKEET

Parakeets, like most birds, tend to hide their illnesses until a disease is quite advanced. A wild parakeet that shows itself to be ill is vulnerable to predators and will try to behave as normally as possible for as long as possible—your parakeet has the same idea. Knowing what to look for in an ailing parakeet will help you to recognize the illness early, which is key to treatment and speedy recovery.

*Excessive sleeping:* An ill parakeet may sleep too much, especially during the day. Sleeping on the bottom of the cage is particularly significant.

*Fluffed up appearance:* If you notice that your parakeet is fluffy, it may be trying to maintain his body temperature and could be fighting off an illness.

*Loss of appetite:* You should know how much food and what types of food your parakeet is consuming each day. If you notice that your bird is not eating or is eating far less than usual, it could be ill.

*Change in attitude:* If your parakeet seems listless and is not behaving in its usual manner, for example, if it has become cranky or limp, call your veterinarian.

*Lameness:* If your parakeet can't use its feet or hold up his head there's something wrong. Possible reasons include injury and egg binding. Consult an avian veterinarian immediately.

*Panting or labored breathing:* These symptoms might signify a respiratory illness or overheating.

*Discharge:* If you notice runniness or discharge on the eyes, nares, or vent, there may be an illness present.

*Change in droppings:* Your parakeet's droppings should consist of a solid green portion, white urates (overlapping the green portion), and a clear liquid. If the droppings are discolored (very dark green, black, yellow, or red) and there has been no change in diet (such as feeding beets or blueberries), there might be a problem. Also, if there's a pungent odor or the droppings seem far more liquid than usual, call your veterinarian immediately.

*Debris around the face or on feathers:* Indicates poor grooming or regurgitation, both of which are potential signs of illness.

*Seizures:* If your parakeet is flailing in its cage and there are no obvious signs of it being caught in parts of its cage or a toy, place it in a smaller, safe container and rush it to your avian veterinarian. This is a very serious condition.

*Severe change in feather quality or quantity:* If your parakeet begins to lose feathers in patches or you notice it picking them out, call your veterinarian for an appointment.

## QUARANTINE

Quarantine is traditionally a period of forty days in which a new bird is kept separate from birds already established in the household—some people choose to shorten this period to thirty days and find no harm in doing so. During the period of quarantine a new bird is watched for signs of illness. You should feed and water the new bird after you care for your other birds and change your clothing and disinfect your hands after any contact with the bird or its cage. Quarantine is the only way to prevent a new bird from passing a potential illness to the birds you already own. It is sometimes not possible to completely separate a new bird from established birds, but you should try to do your best to keep contact at a minimum while the new bird is being quarantined.

**If you bring home a new parakeet, be sure to quarantine it before putting it with your other pets. Look carefully for signs of disease and see your vet if anything turns up.**

## TIPS FOR COMMON EMERGENCIES

Sometimes it's not easy to get to an avian veterinarian right away after an emergency has occurred, so you will have to comfort and treat your parakeet on your own until you can get to the doctor's office. The following is a list of tips for dealing with common emergencies.

### CREATING A HOSPITAL CAGE

A hospital cage is important to have on hand for many emergencies and illnesses. It's a comfortable, warm, safe place for your parakeet to calm down and recuperate from a trauma or sickness. Simply line a ten gallon aquarium with paper towels and place a heating pad on low to medium underneath one half of the aquarium—your bird must be able to move away from the heat if it gets too warm. Cover the aquarium with a mesh aquarium cover and drape a towel over half of the tank. Place a *very* shallow dish of water (a weak bird can drown in even an inch of water) in the cage, as well as some millet spray and seeds or pellets. Do not include toys or perches, but you can include a rolled up hand towel for snuggling. Place the cage in a quiet location and clean the papers once a day or when they become soiled.

### CONTACT WITH POISON

If your bird comes in contact with poison and you notice evidence of vomiting, paralysis, bleeding from the eyes, nares, mouth, or vent, seizures, or shock and you're not able to get to an avian veterinarian right away, call the National Animal Poison Control Center 24-hour Poison Hotline at (800) 548-2423, (888) 4-ANIHELP or (900) 680-0000 and ask for their help. You will need to have an idea of the poison your bird has ingested.

### BROKEN BLOOD FEATHERS

Sometimes a wing or tail feather will break in the middle of the growth process and begin to bleed. This is not a serious injury and is one you can deal with yourself. Keep a styptic powder or pencil on hand in the case of a bleeding emergency and apply the product until the bleeding has stopped. Next, remove the feather with a pair of needle-nosed pliers. While restraining the bird (you may need two people for this procedure), simply grasp the broken feather with the pliers, close to the shaft, and pull straight out. This will stop the bleeding and prevent infection. If you are too squeamish to do this yourself, take your parakeet to your avian veterinarian.

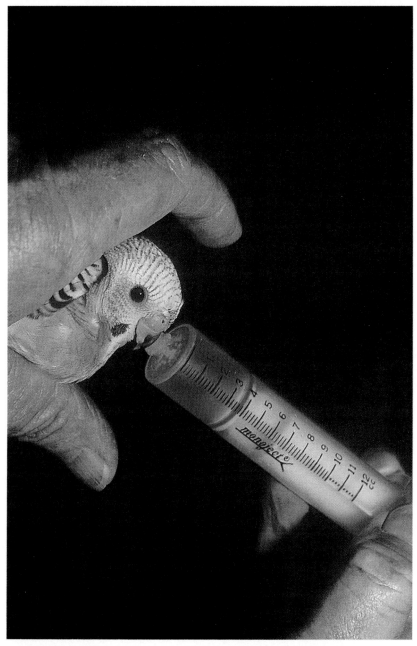

Your veterinarian may give your sick parakeet antibiotics in a food mixture directly by syringe. This method also can be used to give supplements and causes little stress.

## OIL ON THE FEATHERS

If your parakeet becomes soaked in oil it will no longer be able to regulate its body temperature, a condition that can be deadly. Dust the oil-soaked bird with corn starch or flour, then gently bathe it in a small tub of warm water and some mild grease-fighting dish soap. Don't scrub the bird. You may have to repeat this process several times. Keep the bird in a warm hospital cage until most of the oil is removed and the bird is dry.

## IMMEDIATE RESPONSE TO OVERHEATING

An overheated parakeet will pant and spread its wings, trying to cool itself. If this is unsuccessful and the heat does not abate, the bird may lose consciousness and even die. If you notice that your parakeet is becoming overheated, move it immediately to a cooler place and run a fan near its cage. Lightly mist the bird with cool water and offer drops of cool water in its mouth. Never set a parakeet out in the sun unless it has a shady spot to retreat to, and never leave a parakeet in a closed car on a warm day—birds are easily overcome by heat, far quicker than a dog.

## RESPONSE TO EGG BINDING

Occasionally a female parakeet will become calcium deficient or have a disorder of the reproductive tract and an egg will become stuck inside her. This can cause paralysis and even death if left untreated. If you notice your female bird fluffed on the bottom of her cage, panting, and she has a distended belly and her droppings are large and watery, she may be trying to lay an egg. Give her some time to lay it on her own, but if 24 hours pass and she hasn't laid it, you may need to intervene. If you can't get her to an avian veterinarian right away, place a few drops of mineral oil or olive oil in her vent (just at the outside of it) and a couple of drops in her mouth. This may help to lubricate the area and ease the egg out. If that doesn't work, try it again and move her into a very warm hospital cage and call your avian veterinarian. Even if she passes the egg, she might need an examination so that the situation doesn't occur again.

## YOUR PARAKEET'S FIRST AID KIT

Here is a list of essential items for a bird first aid kit. Keep these items in a small tackle box for convenient access when you need them.

Antibiotic ointment (for small wounds, use a non-greasy product only)

### Beyond Good Health

Eyewash

Bandages and gauze

Bottled water

Baby bird formula (can be used for adults having a difficult time eating)

Cotton balls and cotton swabs

Non-greasy first aid lotion

Dishwashing detergent (mild, for cleaning oil off feathers)

Heating pad

Hydrogen peroxide (always use in a weak solution with water)

Nail clippers

Nail file

Needle-nosed pliers (for broken blood feathers)

Penlight

Electrolyte solution, for human babies (for reviving a weak bird)

Saline solution

Sanitary wipes

Sharp scissors

Syringe (without needle)

Styptic powder

Small, clean towels

Spray bottle (for misting)

Alcohol (for sterilizing tools)

Tweezers

Small transport cage

Veterinarian's phone number

A sealed bag or can of your bird's base diet (in case of evacuation)

# Resources

American Budgerigar
Society
1704 Kangaroo
Killeen, Texas 76541

American Federation of
Aviculture
P.O. Box 56218
Phoenix, Arizona 85079-6218
602-484-0931
www.afa.birds.org

Avicultural Society of
America
P.O. Box 5516
Riverside, California 92517-
5517

International Aviculturists
Society
P.O. Box 2232
La Belle, Florida 33975

Association of Avian
Veterinarians
P.O. Box 811720
Boca Raton, Florida 33481
561-393-8901
www.aav.org

# Index

PARAKEETS

## Index

**Photo Credits:**

Dr. Herbert. R. Axelrod: 115
Joan Balzarini: 14; 17; 43; 83; 119
Susan Chamberlain: 29
Isabelle Francais: 12; 13; 21; 25; 34; 36; 41; 44; 46; 56; 62; 77; 78; 88; 96; 98; 99; 103; 107; 112
Michael Gilroy: 10; 32; 35; 60; 61; 63; 67; 94; 111
Eric Ilasenko: 26; 47; 49; 53; 55; 75; 81; 82
Bonnie Jay: 8; 11; 19; 28; 37; 50; 58; 72; 84; 86; 87; 91; 100
Robert Pearcy: 15; 121
Rafi Reyes: 51; 52; 64; 68; 76
John Tyson: 3; 22; 30; 31; 38; 39; 40; 65; 71; 74; 89; 101; 105